A Practical Handbook for Priestly Ministry

Compiled and edited
by Holy Trinity Monastery

Holy Trinity Publications
Holy Trinity Seminary Press
Holy Trinity Monastery
Jordanville, New York
2019

Printed with the blessing of His Eminence,
Metropolitan Hilarion First Hierarch
of the Russian Orthodox Church Outside of Russia

A Practical Handbook for Priestly Ministry
© 2019 Holy Trinity Monastery

HOLY TRINITY
SEMINARY PRESS

An imprint of

HOLY TRINITY PUBLICATIONS
Holy Trinity Monastery
Jordanville, New York 13361-0036
www.holytrinitypublications.com

ISBN: 978-1-942699-24-8 (paperback)
ISBN: 978-1-942699-25-5 (ePub)
ISBN: 978-1-942699-26-2 (Mobipocket)

Library of Congress Control Number 2019939241

Cover Design: James Bozeman.

CONTENTS

Foreword   vii

Preface   ix

Introduction   xiii

Part I: The Instruction of the Parishioners   1

  Chapter 1: Instruction of the People by the Word   3

  Chapter 2: What and Where the Priest Should Teach   9

  Chapter 3: How the Priest Should Teach   15

  Chapter 4: On Instruction by Deed   33

Part II: Ministering the Sacraments   69

  Chapter 5: On the Sacraments in General   71

  Chapter 6: Some Important Aspects of Each Sacrament
              in Particular, Beginning with the Sacrament
              of Holy Baptism   77

  Chapter 7: The Sacrament of Chrismation   81

  Chapter 8: The Sacrament of Confession   83

  Chapter 9: The Sacrament of Holy Communion and Some
              General Remarks Regarding the Serving
              of the Divine Liturgy   99

Chapter 10: The Sacrament of Matrimony 111

Chapter 11: The Sacrament of Unction 115

Part III: On Prayer **119**

Chapter 12: On Prayer in General 121

Chapter 13: How to Pray in Spirit and Truth 129

Chapter 14: Prayer as the Special Duty of Priests 151

Chapter 15: Some Thoughts on Church Style and Its Effect
on the Prayer of the Congregation 167

Concluding Thoughts **171**

Notes **173**

Subject Index **179**

Scripture Index **189**

FOREWORD

In 2011 Holy Trinity Publications published *A Practical Handbook for Divine Services* that provides the clergy and those who serve with them straightforward and detailed guidance for church services, drawing from a number of Russian Orthodox sources.

We are now pleased to offer a complimentary volume *A Practical Handbook for Priestly Ministry* that focuses on pastoral aesthetics and culture. It emphasizes the internal formation and preparation that is an essential prerequisite of the work of the priest.

This book is a compilation of two Russian works. The first is an eighteenth-century classic in its field, "The Treatise on the Duty of Parish Priests," authored by Bishop George (Konissky) of Mogilev (1717–1795) with the assistance of Bishop Parthenius (Sopkovsky) of Smolensk (1717–1795). It was translated into English by Rev. R.W. Blackmore (1791–1882) in 1833 and published as part of a larger volume entitled "The Doctrine of the Russian Church" in 1845. Rev. Blackmore, a graduate of Merton College, Oxford, was an Anglican clergyman who served as chaplain to the Russia Company in Kronstadt. With regard to the "Duty of Parish Priests" Blackmore wrote in his preface that it "has been adopted by the whole Russian Church…and all candidates for holy orders in the Diocesan Seminaries and in the Superior Spiritual Academies are required to have read it, and to shew their acquaintance with its contents, previously to being ordained."

The second source of this compilation is "Pastoral Aesthetics" by Archpriest Alexis Danilovich Ostapov (1930–1975). Fr Alexis, a pupil of His Holiness Patriarch Alexei I of Moscow and All Russia, held a Doctorate of Theology from the Moscow Theological Seminary where he subsequently taught Pastoral Theology, Russian Church History, and Church Archeology as well as other subjects. This text was translated into English by Anthony Williams as part of his studies at Holy Trinity Orthodox Seminary.

Drawing from both of these seminal works, Holy Trinity Publications presents a newly edited and revised handbook suitable for the twenty-first-century pastor and aspirant to the priesthood. This work is replete with detailed quotations from the Holy Fathers and the Canons, together with over one hundred references to Holy Scriptures, covering every conceivable pastoral issue. While we have tried with the greatest care to provide full citations for the scriptural quotations throughout the text, we have not always been able to do the same for those from the Fathers.

We sincerely pray that with its emphasis on the formation of the personality of the ideal Christian pastor—his prayer life, social skills, personal culture, and ability to serve beautifully and with compunction—any priest or aspirant to the priesthood will find this a treasure to be read and reread countless times for instruction and edification. More broadly we hope it will also inspire all, both men and women, who serve in any capacity in the Church to live the kind of life which is at the foundation of all authentic spiritual service.

Holy Trinity Monastery
Paschaltide 2019

PREFACE

There are four duties that priests are bound diligently to fulfill. The first is to preach God's word, without missing a single opportunity, and so to bring their parishioners to the knowledge of the faith and to a good Christian life, according to the injunction of the holy Apostle Paul: "Preach the word! Be ready in season and out of season. Convince, rebuke, exhort, with all longsuffering and teaching" (2 Tim 4:2).

The second is to lead lives in harmony with the doctrine of the Gospel and so to make themselves examples of holiness, "For a bishop must be blameless, as a steward of God, not self-willed, not quick-tempered, not given to wine, not violent, not greedy for money, but hospitable, a lover of what is good, sober-minded, just, holy, self-controlled, holding fast the faithful word as he has been taught, that he may be able, by sound doctrine, both to exhort and convict those who contradict" (Titus 1:7–9).

The third is to minister God's Sacraments, the sole end and aim of which is to confirm those who believe in Christ in faith and in holy living, and so to perfect them for everlasting life and for the kingdom of heaven.

The fourth is to pray to God, which is so profitable and needful to preachers and stewards of the mysteries that without it they can neither preach God's word, nor live holy lives themselves, nor perform the mysteries in a God-pleasing manner. Therefore, according to the apostle's command: Pray without ceasing. They should pray to our gracious God day and night with all their souls and entreat Him to give them the Holy Spirit. For He alone makes men priests and guides them in the performance of their duties into all truth (see John 16:13) and makes them workmen that need not to be ashamed. The Holy Spirit is only given as a result of earnest prayer.

The apostle has clearly shown how important these four duties are by extolling the New Testament above the Old, calling the preaching of the Gospel and stewardship of the mysteries of God the *ministry of the Spirit*, the *ministry of righteousness*, and the *ministry of reconciliation* (see 2 Cor 3:8–9 and 5:18). And everyone can see and understand what skill, wisdom, caution, great piety, faith, and energy—together with the assisting grace of the Holy Spirit—this ministry requires in its stewards, especially considering the commandments regarding the priesthood in the Scriptures and the nature of the Mysteries themselves.

In the Old Testament the Lord through Moses strictly commanded the Priests to be attentive to their ministry: "Tell Aaron and his sons to be careful for the holy things of the children of Israel, in what is sanctified to Me, so as not to defile My holy name: I am the Lord" (Lev 22:2). "You shall keep My Sabbaths and reverence My holy things: I am the Lord" (Lev 19:30).

But if the ministry of the Old Testament needed such strict attention and deep awe in the sight of the Lord, how much more are they needed in the ministry of the New Testament, in the preaching of the Gospel, in the stewardship of the Mysteries, in the ministry of the Spirit, of righteousness, and of reconciliation! The strictest attention and the deepest awe, joined with love and thankfulness, are required of priests.

For if in the priesthood delivered through Moses to Aaron and his sons every disobedience and transgression was punished (see Heb 2:2), how much stricter must the punishment and judgment be for any transgression or neglect in the ministry that has been delivered to the Apostles and to each of us, their successors, by the Lord Jesus Christ Himself? Our Saviour has warned us in His own words when He says that He "will cut [the evil and careless servant] in two and appoint him his portion with the hypocrites" (Matt 24:51).

Therefore, as a priest you must realize that these duties are of no little weight and so require no little skill, wisdom, attention, and piety. The Apostle Paul by his own example at once teaches you this truth and incites you to act on it. For he, while fulfilling the ministry of the Word and Sacraments entrusted to him, writes of himself to the Corinthians thus: "I was with you in weakness, in fear, and in much trembling" (1 Cor 2:3). And in another place he mentions the fear and reverence required for the ministry: "Let us have grace, by which we may serve God acceptably with reverence and godly fear. For our God is a consuming fire" (Heb 12:28–29). Therefore, you must be filled with godly reverence and armed with many skills.

However, we see some priests who do not know their duties, or do not even care to know them, and so give no heed to their calling, but live in great disorder. Lest such be left to the end in their ignorance and carelessness, and so fall under that severity of God's judgment that punished unworthy priests such as Nadab and Abihu, sons of Aaron, and Hophni and Phineas, sons of Eli, in the Old Testament, this book is intended to awaken and instruct such priests. Also, we hope that they who are considering becoming priests, or lesser clergy of the Church, may come to know the greatness and responsibility of the ministry of the New Testament.

Therefore, you priests who bear the name of shepherds receive these instructions with the same zeal with which they were written for you and use them to your profit and that of the souls committed to you. May you not be called the *light of the world* in vain, may you not become blind leaders of the blind, may you not go yourselves headlong, and leading others, into the pit of destruction from where there shall be no deliverance forever.

May God grant you the spirit of wisdom and revelation perfectly to know your duty and to fulfill it. May He enlighten the eyes of your heart to see the riches of the glory prepared for you if you are vigilant to walk in way worthy of your calling and to see what fierce torments, on the other hand, await you if neglect your calling, for if you do, a multitude of souls for whom Christ died will be dragged down together with you into the pit of everlasting perdition. But may He, our Lord Jesus Christ, by His almighty hand save you all from this, deliver you from every evil work, and preserve you for His heavenly kingdom.

INTRODUCTION

The priesthood is a ministry in the New Testament given by Christ to the Apostles and to their successors, consisting in the preaching of the word of God and the ministration of the Sacraments, by these means sinners are reconciled to God and perfected in faith and in holy living unto the attainment of everlasting life, to His glory. Every word of this definition is proved from Holy Scripture in the following chapters.

The priesthood, as has been said, was given in the New Testament by Christ Himself to His disciples and their successors. When He sent the Apostles into the world, He gave them this commandment: "Go therefore and make disciples of all the nations, baptizing them in the name of the Father and of the Son and of the Holy Spirit, teaching them to observe all things that I have commanded you" (Matt 28:19–20). That it was not only to the Apostles but also to their successors, the bishops and priests, that Christ delivered this ministry is evident from His promise, which follows in the same place: "And lo, I am with you always, even to the end of the age." The Apostles themselves did not live to the end of the world, but from the time of the Apostles and even to the end of the world, their successors—the bishops and priests—continue in an uninterrupted succession.

This the Apostle Paul confirms, when he says that Christ Who "ascended on high ... gave some to be apostles, some prophets, some evangelists, and some teachers" (Eph 4:8–11).

The goal and purpose of the priesthood is this—that mankind, who by sin had fallen away from God, and subjected themselves to everlasting punishment, may be brought back again to God's grace and after having been brought back may be so perfected in faith and holy living that being united with Christ, as members with their head, in one body, they may be found worthy to receive eternal life to the glory of the blessed Trinity, the Author, and Accomplisher of our salvation.

With respect to this purpose of priesthood, St Paul calls his apostleship the *ministry of reconciliation* and the preaching of the *word of reconciliation*, that is, of the bringing of sinners to the grace of God (see 2 Cor 5:18–19). And in his Epistle to the Ephesians, after having shown that pastors and teachers are given by Christ, he points out the goal of their ministry: "for the equipping of the saints for the work of ministry, for the edifying of the body of Christ, till we all come to the unity of the faith and of the knowledge of the Son of God, to a perfect man, to the measure of the stature of the fullness of Christ" (Eph 4:12–13).

This makes it sufficiently clear that the priesthood is a great calling, for it was instituted by our Lord Jesus Christ, the God-man, as a means through which men could attain the greatest blessedness— everlasting salvation. The priesthood is further dignified by the titles that the word of God gives to priests. It calls them *messengers of the Lord of Almighty* (Mal 2:7), *Angels of the Churches* (Rev 2:1, 8, 12, 18 and 3:1, 7, 14), the *light of the world* (Matt 5:14, 16), the *salt of the earth* (Matt 5:13), *shepherds of the flock of God* (1 Pet 5:2), *God's fellow workers* and *master builders, God's building* (1 Cor 3:9, 10), the *friends* of Christ (John 15:15).

St John Chrysostom, in his second homily on 2 Timothy, says: "Do you not know what a priest is? He is the Angel of the Lord, for when he speaks according to his office, if you despise him, you despise not him, but the bishop who ordained him, and God."

St Gregory the Theologian, in his second oration, says: "The priest, when he ministers, stands with the angels, glorifies God with the archangels, lifts up sacrifice to the heavenly altar on high, is joined as a priest with Christ, renews our corrupt dust, restores the image of God." In other words, he brings fallen man by baptism to regeneration.

St John Chrysostom, in his third book *On the Priesthood* (ch. IV), also says: "The priesthood is conferred on earth, but it has the rank of heavenly things. And this is said with the strictest truth, for it was not a man, nor an angel, nor an archangel, nor any other created power, but the Comforter Himself, the Holy Spirit, Who appointed this order and taught men, while still living in the flesh, to imitate the ministry of angels."

But since the priesthood is of such great dignity, it is no slight labor but a very great one, as will become further obvious in a detailed description of its duties. Indeed, the very names that Holy Scripture uses to designate the labors, the watching, the patience, and the exercises required of a pastor, suffice to let every one know this.

Chrysostom, in his fifteenth homily on 1 Timothy, writes:

The Law commands not to muzzle the ox that treads out the corn. Can you not see what labors it requires from the teacher? For there is no labor, no, not one, like this labor. Let us not think only of the hire, but of that qualification that is joined with the command, for it goes on: The laborer is worthy of his hire. And so, if any one gives himself up to indulgence and ease, he is not worthy. If he is not the ox that treads, if he stands not against frost and briars, and does not plough the land or work it without resting until he gathers the harvest into the granary: he is not worthy.

Chrysostom, in his second book *On the Priesthood* (ch. IV) and in his tenth moral on 1 Thessalonians and his third moral on the Acts of the Apostles, enlarges on the difficulties and dangers of the pastoral calling. And St Gregory the Great, writing of the burden of the priesthood, says that "for a Priest to know how to rule well the flock committed to him, is a science above all sciences, and an art above all arts."

The dignity of the priesthood and the difficulties of the pastoral office can result in very grave dangers, for the higher and more rewarding the order—if well ministered—the more vile and wretched must be any misconduct in it, especially sloth, and the more doomed to the fiercest torments (see Matt 24:48–51; 25:30).

The Apostle Paul when committing this fearful and dangerous dignity to his successors charged and instructed them to keep it "before God and the Lord Jesus Christ, who will judge the living and the dead at His appearing and His kingdom" (2 Tim 4:1) and before the elect angels, the zealous executors of God's judgment (see 1 Tim 5:21).

His strong sense of the dangers of the priesthood moved St John Chrysostom to utter the fearful words found in his Homilies: "I do not think there are many priests who will be saved, but the greater part will perish" (third moral on Acts).

This dignity, difficulty, and danger of the priesthood should be constantly before the eyes of all who aspire to it, so that they may first examine themselves to see whether they can bear such a burden, whether they have the necessary spiritual powers and qualifications, such as understanding, learning, skill in speech, good morals, a blameless and exemplary life, all of which the apostle requires in a priest (1 Tim 3 and Titus 1). For even priests who possess, such virtues become guilty of sin if they are unwilling to serve God and their neighbor, especially when called to do so, but those who do not possess these virtues, not only should they avoid taking upon themselves this calling, like the false prophets, but even if they are called, even if they are pressed to enter it, they should refuse.[1]

But above all let him who would approach the priesthood ask his own heart, whether it feels Christ saying to him "Do you love me? .... Feed My lambs" and whether it answers this question with St Peter without guile, "Lord, You know that I love you" (John 21:15). He should ask himself if he goes into the sheepfold for the sake of the sheep that they may have life or for his own gain that he may rob, kill, and destroy (John 10:10). If with the former purpose he enters in by the door, he is a shepherd, but if with the latter he climbs in some other way and is a thief and a robber.

The duties of the priesthood consist principally in teaching, living a holy life, ministering the Sacraments, and praying for the people.

Teaching and ministering the Sacraments are clearly pointed out by the apostle, when he says, "Let a man so consider us, as servants of

Christ and stewards of the mysteries of God" (1 Cor 4:1). Living a holy life is as Christ Himself points out: "Let your light so shine before men, that they may see your good works..." (Matt 5:16). Praying for people is a duty that is enjoined by the Lord in the Old Testament (Lev 16:34 and Joel 2:17), by the Apostle Paul in his first Epistle to Timothy 2:1–2, by St James (see James 5:14), and in Acts 6:4. But of this we shall speak more at length in Part IV.

PART I

The Instruction of the Parishioners

CHAPTER 1

Instruction of the People by the Word

The priest is called to serve God as a minister of the altar. A vital component of this calling is to share with the bishop in the teaching of the people. Our Saviour Jesus Christ Himself has shown that it is a particular and indispensable duty of the priest (as well as the bishop) to teach the people, since He gave a commandment to the Apostles not only to baptize but also to teach, and first to teach, afterwards to baptize (see Matt 28:19 and Mark 16:15–16). Teaching should precede the administration of Sacraments: for Sacraments without faith profit the receiver nothing, but faith cannot be without a preacher (Rom 10:14). And do not say, if you are a priest, that this command was given to the Apostles, not to me. You are the successor of the Apostles in the work of baptism; therefore, also in the work of teaching, and it has been shown already that when Jesus Christ gave the commandment to His Apostles to teach and baptize, He gave it to all bishops, and to all priests likewise, even to the end of the world.

The Apostle Paul said the same when he exclaimed of himself, groaning, "Woe is me! if I preach not the gospel, For if I do this willingly, I have a reward" (1 Cor 9:16–17). He wrote the same when he charged Timothy Bishop of Ephesus, instructing him by God and by the awful judgment of Christ to "Preach the word! Be ready in season and out of season. Convince, rebuke, exhort, with all longsuffering and teaching" (2 Tim 4:1–2). Lastly, he wrote it when he required from every priest, without exception, that he be *able to teach* (2 Tim 2:24). Indeed, three whole Epistles of his, two to Timothy and one to Titus, are filled with the most earnest charges and the most insistent commandments to the performance of this duty (1 Tim 4:6, 14; 6:6:2 and 2 Tim 2:2, 14–15, 24:3:4; 4:5 and Titus 2:1, 7, 15; 3:8).[2] Not only does the Lord require pastors to teach God's people, but He enforces this duty with the severest threatening: under pain of having the blood of them that perish on the hands of the pastors, under penalty of the fiercest torments, prepared for all slothful servants and stewards. "Son of man, I have made you a watchman for the house of Israel; therefore hear a word from My mouth, and give them warning from Me: When I say to the wicked, 'You shall surely die,' and you do not give him explicit warning, nor speak to warn the lawless to turn from his ways, so he may live, that lawless man shall die in his unrighteousness; but his blood I will require at your hand" (Ezek 3:17–18). Similar threats are found in chapters 33:8 and 34:10. In the New Testament He says: "The master of that servant will come on a day when he is not looking for him and at an hour that he is not aware of, and will cut him in two and appoint him his portion with the hypocrites. There shall be weeping and gnashing of teeth" (Matt 24:50–51).

As you read this, pay attention, if you are a priest! The Lord has adorned you with the grace of the priesthood. You must endeavor then to be worthy of this grace in your actions. You are called an *Angel* of the Lord of Hosts; therefore, you are undoubtedly bound to proclaim to men the will and law of the Lord of Hosts, for the word "angel" means "herald," and it is for this reason that the priest is called an angel—*his lips*, as a fountain, *should keep knowledge*, and the "people should seek the law from his mouth" (Mal 2:7). You are called a pastor or Shepherd; feed, therefore, the flock committed to you; defend those who are attacked; heal those who are sick; call back those who stray. But you can only feed your flock by instruction, as it is written by the prophet: "I will give you shepherds according to My heart, and they will thoroughly shepherd you with knowledge" (Jer 3:15). Likewise, you can only defend and heal by the word of God, which is our whole armory (2 Cor 10:4 and Eph 5:17 and Heb 4:12 and Prov 30:5). It is "the power of God to salvation for everyone who believes" (Rom 1:16), the wisdom of God, "which [is] able to make you wise for salvation" (2 Tim 3:15); it is a medicine to the sick, a *path* to them that are gone astray (Ps 118:35). You are the *overseers* of the flock committed to you (Acts 20:28). You are made as a "watchman for the house of Israel" (Ezek 33:7).

"Father" is the title by which you are customarily addressed; therefore, be a father to your parishioners in your actions, making them children of God by preaching the Gospel and by ministering the Sacraments (1 Cor 4:15). Have also the compassion of a mother toward them, *laboring in birth* with Paul, "until Christ is formed in [them]" (Gal 4:19). You are the servant of the King, sent to call them that are bidden to the wedding of His Son (Matt 22:3), to the great supper (Luke 14:17). Not a servant only but the *friend of the bridegroom* (John 3:29) and the one who presents the bride to Christ (2 Cor 11:2). Call then; do not walk around in silence. You must always go about to ask, entreat, compel your parishioners to come in that the house of the Lord may be filled with guests: betroth your flock to one husband so that you may "present [it] as a chaste virgin to Christ" (2 Cor 11:2).

The pastors of the first ages of Christianity had this duty deeply engraved in their hearts, and they did not fail to warn us of the consequences of neglecting it. To this end, they enforced it by canons in both the ecumenical and local councils, and in their writings and instructions continually and earnestly inculcated its importance in all who should take upon themselves this calling: "If any Bishop, upon his appointment, through sloth neglect to teach, let him be suspended, until he amend.[3] If any Bishop, or Priest, be neglectful of his inferior Clergy and people, and fail to instruct them in the faith, let him be suspended; and if he remain still in his negligence, let him be deposed.[4] Let the elders, that is, the Bishop and Priest of the Church, every day, but especially on all Sundays, teach the people God's commandments; and let them speak not of their own private spirit, but according to the sense of the Holy Fathers."[5] Furthermore, St Gregory the Theologian, in his First Oration, says the following: "Of all episcopal and priestly duties, the very first is that of preaching the word of God." St John Chrysostom, in his second homily on the Epistle to Titus, has no other name for the place or chair of the bishop than this: *the place of teaching.* In his tenth homily on the Epistle to the Romans, he says, "This is my Priesthood: to preach and proclaim the Gospel."

There remains now no more room for doubt on this first and most important of priestly duties, but only for wonder and grief of heart, that with many of us it is commonly reckoned either as their last duty or as no duty at all. Wherefore such should tremble, lest of them be spoken that word of the Prophet Jeremiah: "The priests did not say, 'Where is the Lord?' And those who handle the law did not know Me; The rulers also transgressed against Me" (Jer 2:8 (NKJV)). They should fear too the judgment of the Lord that condemns the slothful and wicked servant who "hid [his] talent in the ground" (Matt 25:25). To this judgment refer certain images through which the Apostles (2 Pet 2:17 and Jude 12) designate slothful and dissolute teachers, calling them *wells without water, late autumn trees without fruit, twice dead,* while the Prophet Isaiah reproaches such as *blind* and *dumb* (Isa 56:10).

The aforementioned sloth and the ignorance blamed by the Prophet Jeremiah encourage nearly all pastors to "seek their own, not the things which are of Christ Jesus" (Phil 2:21). In other words, they care for themselves, not for the salvation of the people. And they do even worse than this when, leaving the word of God, they incline to superstitious fables and "do not hold fast the pattern of sound words" (2 Tim 1:13); rather, they speak vain things and so lead their parishioners into superstition and schism.

Here for their instruction priests should notice the following words of the Lord:

> Son of man, prophesy against the shepherds of Israel; prophesy and say to the shepherds, "Thus says the Lord and Master: 'O shepherds of Israel who feed themselves, should not the shepherds feed the sheep? Behold you drink the milk and clothe yourselves with the wool. You slay the fatlings, but do not feed My sheep. You have not strengthened the weak, and the sick you have not revived. The broken you have not bandaged, and the misled you have not brought back. The lost you have not sought, and the strong you have not prepared for labor.' ... Thus says

the Lord and Master: 'Behold, I am against the shepherds, and shall require My sheep at their hands. I shall turn them away so they may not shepherd My sheep. The shepherds will not feed them anymore, for I shall deliver My sheep from their mouth; and they shall no longer be as food for them.'" (Ezek 34:2–4, 10)

"Woe to the shepherds who scatter and destroy the sheep of My pasture!" (Jer 23:1). This entire chapter in Jeremiah is a terrifying injunction to priests, and it is extremely instructive to read it together with Ezekiel chapter 13, from verse 18 to the end.

Lest any of you fall into such sloth and into such dangerous ignorance or lest he who has been guilty of these already remain in this sin to the end, two things are recommended. First, we exhort you to read over these sections frequently and to bear in mind and meditate on the Scriptures referred to in them. Second, you must pray most sincerely and with genuine faith to Jesus Christ our Lord that He may always guide us by the Holy Spirit and lead us into all truth.

These two methods will be, as it were, two most useful medicines, for to such as are in health they will act to strengthen and preserve the soundness of their reason and will, while to the sick they will be medicines of healing. For the words of the Lord make those who receive them "wise for salvation through faith which is in Christ Jesus. All Scripture is given by inspiration of God, and is profitable for doctrine, for reproof, for correction, for instruction in righteousness, that the man of God may be complete, thoroughly equipped for every good work" (2 Tim 3:15–17). But all these things will only then become a part of our inner life when we pray to the Lord with heartfelt faith, for through prayer our "heavenly Father [gives] the Holy Spirit to those who ask Him" (Luke 11:13). We are strongly assured of the truth of this by our Saviour Jesus Christ Himself (see John 14:13–14 and 15:7).

CHAPTER 2

What and Where the Priest Should Teach

It is the priest's duty to teach his flock the faith and the law, the word "law" here meaning the good works of the law. Christ Himself taught us these two things and therefore began His preaching thus: "Repent, and believe in the gospel" (Mark 1:15). And the Apostle Paul in like manner taught both Jews and Greeks "repentance toward God, and faith toward our Lord Jesus Christ" (Acts 20:21). Repentance here indicates the works of the law, and the Gospel indicates faith in Christ.

This may be clearly seen from all St Paul's Epistles, in which the apostle first proposes the doctrine of the faith and then writes of the good works of the law, exhorting Christians to "walk worthy of [their] calling" (Eph 4:1), that is to "live soberly, righteously, and godly in the present age … denying ungodliness and worldly lusts" (Titus 2:12–13). Indeed all Holy Scripture, both the Old and the New Testaments, has the same subject, and the Holy Fathers of the Church, following the word of God, have always taught faith and holy living according to the law; consequently, it is the duty of every priest in the work of his calling to do the same.

The faith consists in various tenets, which Christians must believe and confess, some of which refer to dogmatic truth and so are necessary to salvation, because without their knowledge one cannot be saved, any more than a person can live without the principal parts of his body, such as the head and the heart. Others, especially for simple people busied with worldly callings, are less necessary, since they are implied in the first and are only their more precise explanation.

To the first class of tenets belongs the mystery of the Holy Trinity, the mission of the Son of God into the world, our justification by His death, God's mercy to fallen man, His Grace leading to repentance, and the like. Tenets of the second class include the doctrine of the predestination of the righteous and the wicked—the latter to destruction, the first to everlasting life—the justification of those who lived under the former dispensation that is the Old Testament and so forth.

All the tenets of our faith are contained in the word of God, that is, in the books of the Old and New Testaments, and they are systematically described by dogmatic theology, with which the pastor, who must teach others, must be well acquainted.

The tenets of the faith that are strictly necessary for salvation have been collected from the Scriptures in the Councils of Nicaea and Constantinople and put together into one form called the Symbol of Faith, or the Creed. But they are more fully and systematically set forth in books of a catechetical format, from which all priests, especially such as have not studied theology, are absolutely bound, first thoroughly to inform themselves and then to teach all their parishioners.[6]

The Ten Commandments are likewise contained in Holy Scripture (in the twentieth chapter of Exodus) and since they are innate in us—the mirror of that image of God in which man was created—every Christian without exception is most certainly required to know them and to lead his life by them, doing good works and shunning evil.

Since the tenets of our faith and the Ten Commandments are contained in Holy Scripture, it follows, beyond dispute, that we hold the word of God, that is, the books of the Old and New Testaments, as the source, foundation, and perfect rule both of our holy faith and of the good works of the law. Therefore, it is our duty to search the word of God and draw from it divine truth to teach the people,[7] to confirm our own words from the word of God,[8] and to test all doctrine that either we ourselves may hear from others or others from us by the truth of the Scriptures, receiving what is conformable to them and rejecting what is contrary. This is evident both from God's own words, and from the canons of the Councils and the teaching of the Holy Fathers.[9]

St Athanasius the Great, in the thirty-ninth of his Epistles on the Feasts, toward the end, after having enumerated the books of the Old and New Testaments, says the following: "These books are the well-springs of salvation: from these, if any one thirsts, let him draw the words of God. In these alone is the doctrine of the true faith preached. Let no one add anything to these, nor take anything away. Out of these books the Lord put the Sadducees to shame, saying: Ye do err, not knowing the Scriptures, while He taught the Jews thus: Search the Scriptures."

St Basil the Great, in his Short Canons, in reply to the First Question—"Whether it be profitable or possible to do any good thing, or speak, or think of ourselves, without the testimony of the divinely-inspired Scriptures?"—answers thus: "Our Lord Jesus Christ said of the Holy Spirit, that He does not speak by Himself, but whatever He shall hear, that shall He speak, and of Himself He says the following: The Son can do nothing by Himself; and again: I have not spoken of Myself, but the Father Which sent Me, He gave Me a commandment what I should say, and what I should speak, and so on. Therefore, much more we, who always need the Holy Spirit as our guide and teacher in the way of truth, should determine both our reasoning and our word, and our deeds by the Word of God." The same Father, in his Morals, Canon 26, chapter 1, says, "The teacher should confirm every word and thing by the witness of the Divinely-inspired Scripture, for the more perfect confirmation of the truth, and for the confounding of error."

Furthermore, St Basil, in his Morals, Canon 72, tells us to "test all doctrine proposed to us by other teachers, and if it is conformable to the Divine Scriptures, then receive it, but if it is contrary, reject it and turn away from such teachers." For the same reasons, St Ambrose, in his "On Faith" (Chapter 7), calls the Holy Scripture "the priest's own book," and St Dionysius the Areopagite, in the first chapter of his book on the Divine Hierarchy, calls the Scriptures "the very essence of priesthood."

That we ought to test all doctrine by the word of God is also seen from the following testimony: "Test all things, hold fast what is good. Abstain from every form of evil" (1 Thess 5:21–22). "Do not believe every spirit, but test the spirits, whether they are of God, because many false prophets have gone out into the world" (1 John 4:1). "Even if we, or an angel from heaven, preach any other gospel than what we have preached to you, let him be accursed" (Gal 1:8).

Basil the Great in his Morals, Canon lxxii., bids us prove any doctrine that may be proposed to us by other teachers—to check if it be agreeable to the Divine Scriptures, then to receive it, but if it be contrary, to reject it and to turn away from such teachers. For just the same reasons, St Ambrose calls the Holy Scripture the priest's own book, and Dionysius the Areopagite calls it the very essence of priesthood.[10]

The Fathers of the Church confirm this—Athanasius the Great, in his thirty-ninth Epistle on the Feasts and in his Synopsis of the Old and New Testaments, St Gregory the Theologian, in his poetry, St Amphilochius, Bishop of Iconium, in his *Iambics to Seleucius*, and St John of Damascus, in his fourth book on the Faith (Chapter 17), have listed by name all the books of both Testaments—and have taught us the same doctrine respecting them. And all the other Fathers of the Church, whenever they say in their writings that the word of God, or Holy Scripture, teaches us this or that, mean nothing else by Scripture, but the writings of the Old and New Testaments.[11]

The text of the above-mentioned books is not simply human, but it was written by revelation and command of God, by the Holy Spirit. The Apostle Peter says, "No prophecy of Scripture is of any private interpretation, for prophecy never came by the will of man, but holy men of God spoke as they were moved by the Holy Spirit" (2 Pet 1:20–21). And the Apostle Paul says, "The gospel which was preached by me is not according to man. For I neither received it from man, nor was I taught it, but it came through the revelation of Jesus Christ" (Gal 1:11–12). The Epistle to the Hebrews says the same thing: "God Who at various times, and in various ways spoke ... " (Heb 1:1).

Past events were thus revealed, such as the creation of the world to Moses, as well as future events, both to him and to the other prophets, by God alone. "For who will declare the things from the beginning, that we may also know the former things and say they are true?" (Isa 41:26). The things that have been from the beginning who shall declare unto us? I have declared and have saved. The same prophets were ordered by the Lord also to write what they heard: "Write this for a memorial in the book" (Exod 17:14) (see also Isa 30:8 and Jer 30:2). And in the New Testament: "Write the things which you have seen, and the things which are, and the things which will take place after this" (Rev 1:19).

But the things committed to writing in the above-named Testaments surpass all human reason. Let any one seriously consider the creation of the world, its order, the miracles performed in Egypt, at the Red Sea, and in the Wilderness, the Incarnation of Jesus Christ the Son of God, His miracles, the Resurrection from the dead, the outpouring of the Holy Spirit on the Apostles, and the conversion of the Gentiles by their preaching to Christ. All these answer not to the reason or power of man, nor any other creature, but to the Almighty power and unsearchable wisdom of God alone. And thus, both the writing of the text itself and the things written there, and the fulfillments of prophecies give us the strongest and most incontrovertible assurance that the Old and New Testaments are indeed the word of God.

A priest's study of these Scriptures must become a constant unveiling to himself of more and more of the ways of understanding this eternal book. This is reached through constant attentive reading, coupled with prayer and contemplation, and also through reading the commentaries and excellent sermons of the Holy Fathers.

I repeat that the writings of the Holy Fathers are of great use, for they contain either the very same tenets of the faith explained from the word of God, or instructions for holy living, or canons and rules for the discipline and good order of the Church and of the whole Christian community, which we collectively call the traditions of the Church. Therefore, we both may and on sometimes must quote the writings of the Holy Fathers in our sermons, including any passages as may be suitable for the explanation of any tenet of the faith, or to confirm the doctrine we deliver to the people. But neither the writings of the Holy Fathers nor the traditions of the Church are to be confounded or equaled with the word of God and His commandments, for the word of God is one thing but the writings of the Holy Fathers and Church Tradition is another.[12]

Here it will not be out of place to mention the distinction that St Basil the Great lays down between the Lord's commandments and traditions. "In our time many men openly neglect our Saviour's commandments, while they follow rather the traditions of men. To live in mountains and deserts, to shut oneself up in a cell, to eat only once in the day, to refrain altogether even from bread and water, to wear sackcloth, and the like, is the tradition of holy men devised for good, but they who do these things ought first to keep the Lord's commandments—those of long-suffering and truth, humility and temperance, forgetfulness of injuries and indifference to worldly things, faith, patience, and charity unfeigned, without which it is impossible to please God ... For me, if anyone keep not these commandments of the Lord, but swear and lie, and slander, and rejoice at what is amiss in others, I receive him not, no, not even if he lives his whole life in sackcloth and ashes, and abstains from every single kind of food."[13] And in another place St Basil writes thus: "Fasting and watching, and lying on the ground, and anything else that is done without the law of the Lord, Christ will receive, for they are the traditions of holy men, but He will not punish any who for their bodily weakness neglect such things. But of His own commandments He has said, that He will disown and punish with torments all who of slothfulness transgress ..."[14]

CHAPTER 3

How the Priest Should Teach

There are five principal avenues by which a priest discharges his duty to teach his parishioners:

1. By expounding the faith, and perfecting his parishioners in it day by day.
2. By refuting and rooting out all heretical, impious, or superstitious doctrine contrary to the faith.
3. By correcting and bringing back such as have fallen into sin.
4. By guiding and confirming in holy living the faithful and well disposed.
5. By comforting and restoring them who are in sorrow and despair.

This fivefold distinction of the kinds of duties of teaching was laid down by the Apostle Paul when he wrote: "All Scripture is given by inspiration of God, and is profitable for doctrine, for reproof, for correction, for instruction in righteousness, that the man of God may be complete, thoroughly equipped unto all good works" (2 Tim 3:16–17). "For whatever things were written before were written for our learning, that we through patience and comfort of the Scriptures might have hope" (Rom 15:4). Also bear in mind the words of God in Ezekiel (34:4) where the Lord rebukes the careless shepherds and lists the different ways of tending the flock.

With regard to the first kind: if the priest while he teaches his people the faith finds that they do not learn from his doctrine, he should remember that he must not burden them with high and difficult theological treatises on doctrines nor with words needing much explanation. It is enough to teach them those tenets of the faith that are strictly necessary for salvation, explaining them in few plain and simple words, and proving them by one or two passages from the word of God, nor should he stop explaining any one tenet until it is clearly understood and correctly repeated by his parishioners.

At the same time, it must be remembered that the intellectual level of our parishioners and inquirers is growing: their knowledge and questions are increasingly more complicated. Therefore, the pastor must be more accomplished, more spiritually experienced than his flock; his knowledge of the Church must not be lower but much higher than that of those who inquire. Woe to that pastor whose parishioners are more churched, more spiritual, more humane, and more cultured than he is.

The priest may teach by question and answer, both for the easier understanding of others and that he may himself be able to examine his hearers and determine whether they have understood what has been said or not. This method of teaching was commonly used by the ancient Fathers of the Church.

Since faith always has for its end godliness, according to that command of the apostle "exercise yourself toward godliness" (1 Tim 4:7), it will be very much to the purpose, and very profitable, if the priest, as he teaches the tenets of the faith, draws from them specific instructions that may help his parishioners lead a Christian life.

When the priest explains the dogma of the faith that *God is Spirit* (John 4:24), he should lead his parishioners to the understanding that worship and the sacrifice offered to Him must therefore also be spiritual (see Rom 12:1). This means that outward or bodily worship and material sacrifices, such as candles, incense, and other offerings and devotions, without spiritual piety and good living cannot be agreeable to Him (Isa 1:11–12, 17).

Here are some other examples. When the priest teaches his parishioners that *God is everywhere present, and fillest all things*[15], he should help them come to the understanding that we can nowhere hide our sins from Him. When he teaches that God *by grace*, through the name of His Son, forgives those who believe in Him their sins, they should infer that we are so much the more bound to keep His commandments, as it is written in the Epistle to the Ephesians 2:8–10. Other tenets of the faith can be explained in a similar fashion, and the people will soon learn to live holily and to believe correctly, and both faith and law will be more firmly rooted in their minds.

Furthermore, every instruction should be accompanied by fervent prayer to God, following the apostle's example in Ephesians 1:16–17. The priest must pray that God will open the mind and heart of the hearers to understand and receive His word (Luke 24:45, Acts 16:14), that the seed sown in them will not remain without fruit, that it will not be devoured by evil birds or choked by the thorns of the cares of this life (Matt 13:22), that the word, which is the instrument of our salvation, will not become to them a greater condemnation by rendering them speechless at the judgment (John 12:48; 15:22). Therefore, he should also exhort his hearers that they should pray with the same petitions to God both in their own houses and in secret.

As for the better educated, especially in city parishes, it has been customary for a long time to teach them with formal homilies, the composition of which depends on the customary rules of rhetoric and a special course of instruction, which they who want to become skilled in preaching must take special care to learn. In the composition and delivery of their sermons, preachers of the word of God should be very careful not to make praise, honor, or any other personal advantage the purpose of their labors but only the glory of God and the edification of the parishioners, according to the words of the Apostle Paul: "For our exhortation did not come from error or uncleanness, nor was it in deceit. But as we have been approved by God to be entrusted with the gospel, even so we speak, not as pleasing men, but God who tests our hearts. For neither at any time did we use flattering words, as you know, nor a cloak for covetousness—God is witness. Nor did we seek glory from men, either from you or from others … So, affectionately longing for you, we were well pleased to impart to you not only the gospel of God, but also our own lives" (1 Thess 2:3–6, 8).

St John Chrysostom, in his sixth book *On the Priesthood*, says, "Let not the preacher, who has taken upon himself the labor of instruction, strive for outward popularity, for it degrades his soul. But let this intent alone let him compose his discourses—that they be God-pleasing. Let this be his sole rule and measure of excellence in their composition, not the applause or praise of men. Should it so chance that he be praised of men also, let him not reject their praise, but when he meets with no praise from his hearers, let him not seek it, nor be vexed, for this is comfort enough for him in his labors, and the greatest of all comforts, to be conscious within himself that he has composed his sermon to please God, and in his teaching looks solely to Him." In his Eighth Sermon on Ephesians, he writes: "It is the virtue of teachers not to seek honor or glory from their hearers, but their salvation, and to use all diligence for this: for whoever seeks glory is not a teacher, but a tormentor."

St Gregory the Great, in his Homilies on the Priesthood, says: "The adulterer does not seek offspring, but the gratification of his lust. In the same way, the preacher who is led captive by vainglory, may justly be called an adulterer with the word of God, for by preaching he seeks not to beget children to God, but to boast in his own eloquence."

With regard to the second kind of teaching, that is, the refutation of heretics, if any wolf show himself without or if any of the sheep have sucked the wolf's milk of heretics and infidels, and so has become a wolf and begins to tear the other sheep from the saving fold of Christ's Church with soul-destroying doctrine, the pastor should at first deal with him privately, showing him with clear and strong proofs his errors. But if he remains obstinate, and there is no hope of his conversion nor any other means to recover him to the true way, and rather the danger of his drawing others after him grows more imminent, then the pastor should publicly, in the church, without naming or in any way bringing attention to the person, expose the heresy and all that is contrary to Christ's doctrine in it, and refute it with clear and solid examples from the word of God and the works of the Holy Fathers but without attacking the heretic directly (2 Tim 2:24–25), for this will not bring an adversary to the knowledge of the truth, but only make him more bitter, more fierce, and more blind.

At the same time, the priest should admonish all the faithful not to listen to any soul-destroying doctrine, but as far as possible, in obedience to the apostle's command, they should turn away from the heretic (Titus 3:10). Augustine, in his Commentary on the Gospel of St. John, says, "The wolf has already seized the sheep by the throat; the devil has taught heresy to him that was orthodox; and you are silent. You do not forbid him; you fear to provoke him. O hireling! You saw the wolf, and you fled. Perhaps you will say, No, I am here. Here indeed you are, but you flee in that you are silent."

Such reproof should certainly be done with zeal (Titus 1:13), but zeal according to God, proceeding not from enmity or any other passion—as in the case of false apostles (Gal 4:17)—but from earnestness for God's glory and for the salvation of mankind. Moreover, this zeal should be reasonable and guarded, for blind zeal, even if intended to please God, is rejected (Luke 9:54, Rom 10:2). Still less should it be that hypocritical zeal that shows itself in times of peace as a lion, but in times of danger as a hare. At the same time, it should not be without meekness (2 Tim 2:24–25; 2 Thess 3:15), which will go excellently well together with zeal, if while the pastor is warm and vehement against heresy, his heart is wounded for the persons that err, thereby quenching the thunder of his words with his tears.[16]

Canon LXVI of the Council of Carthage has these words: "It is fit to use meekness and humility in addressing the Donatists (or any heretics and schismatics, for that matter) and conferring with them, though they cut themselves off from the Church; that so beholding our great meekness, they may be ashamed, and return from the bondage of error."[17]

The third kind of teaching, as has been shown above, is the correction of those who live wicked and disordered lives, and this kind requires so much more caution and prudence than the rest, as the office of the physician is more difficult with the sick than with the healthy. And first, with regard to those who live disordered lives, the priest should begin by dealing privately with the party alone, in the same manner as has been described above with regard to such as have fallen into heresy, especially if the disorders of the person have not yet come to be publicly known in the Church (Matt 18:15–16). But if private admonitions do not inspire his conversion, and the disorder becomes notorious, or if there are many at once infected with the same sin, it is proper for the spiritual physician to deal publicly and generally, taking care duly to proportion the remedy to the disease (1 Tim 5:20), yet not expressly to expose the guilty parties themselves, but only to reveal the severity, foulness, and gravity of the wound that he is treating.

Chrysostom, in his second book *On the Priesthood*, says: "A pastor should have much discretion, and eyes innumerable, to enable him to survey on all sides the state of the soul. For as there are many who throw away all hope of amendment, and fall into despair of salvation from not being able to endure sharp treatment, so on the other hand there are some, who if they meet with no discipline adequate to their disorders, become contemptuous and careless, and so are made worse than before, and run to greater lengths of sin. For we must leave nothing untried, but after diligently considering all circumstances, we must apply the treatment that is suitable for the case."[18] The same Father, in a homily on Matthew 18, says: "Sin is either open, or secret. If open, let it be openly rebuked; if secret, then the right thing is brotherly admonition between you and the guilty party in private."

Blessed Augustine says, "If you knowest that your brother has sinned against you, and you seek to rebuke him before all, you are not a teacher, but a betrayer. What is this, "has sinned against you?" You know that he hath sinned, but since it was in secret, when he sinned against you, you must seek a secret place to rebuke him for his sin."

When correcting sinful living, it is important to keep the following in mind:

1. The difference between willful and involuntary sin, deliberate sins and sins of ignorance or infirmity, in particular the enormity of willful sin is that it draws down the sinner straight into the pit of hell (Num 15:27–30). Willful sin often develops into the unforgiveable sin that resists the Holy Spirit and the influence of His grace (Heb 6:4. 9; 10:26 and 1 John 5:16). We must also remember

the power of habitual sin, its dominion over the sinner, and the difficulty of deliverance from it.

2. To show the connection of one sin with another and how quickly men progress from one transgression to another.

3. To set before the eyes of sinners the wrath of God, the approaching judgment, which shall be terrible even to the righteous, the loss of the happiness of heaven, the inheritance of torments in hell, and their eternal duration.

4. Finally, to teach the meaning of true repentance, and that it should be continued not only until after confession, but to the very hour of death, even if the penance imposed by the confessor is only of short duration. But of this more shall be said later when we write at greater length about the Sacrament of Confession.

But if anywhere, then certainly here and among us, more than among all other people, the word of reproof should be spoken with godly zeal. Every priest must have these words of God sounding in his ears: "Cry aloud with strength, and spare not; lift up your voice like a trumpet, and declare to My people their sins" (Isa 58: 1), as well as the commandment of Paul to Timothy: "Preach the word! Be ready in season and out of season. Convince, rebuke, exhort" (2 Tim 4:2). But if here the pastor is ashamed to reprove, or what is worse, is even complicit in the sin—and so, as God says by the Prophet, "'Peace, peace' and there is no peace" (Ezek 13: 10) or thundering only at the poor and mean while flattering the rich and noble—such a pastor is not the physician of his sheep, but their murderer.

St John Chrysostom, in his homily on the first chapter of Galatians, says, "To speak forever mildly to one's hearers when they need sharpness is not the act of a teacher, but of a destroyer and an enemy. Therefore, the Lord, though He said many things to His disciples mildly, sometimes used harsh expressions. He said to Peter, 'Blessed are you, Simon, Bar-Jona,' and promised to lay the foundation of the Church on his confession, but afterwards He said, 'Get behind Me, Satan; you are an offence to Me.' And again, in another place, "Are you also still without understanding?'" (Matt 15:16).

But we must be careful not to place "a piece of unshrunk cloth on an old garment," because "the tear is made worse" (Matt 9:16). It is quite necessary for our teaching, rebuke, and exhortation to be tempered by the spirit of meekness and patience. (Gal 6:1–2; 2 Tim 2:25). Certainly the pastor who follows Christ will not pour something painful into fresh wounds, but rather a soothing wine and oil (Luke 10:34). For he cannot do otherwise—if he has the compassion of a father and of a mother, as he ought to have (1 Thess 2:11)—than grieve with St Paul over sinners (Gal 4:19; 2 Cor 11:29) and wash their wounds, like the same apostle and other true pastors of old, not only in the church but also in his private prayer with his tears (Acts 20:19, 31 and 2 Cor 2:4; 12:21 and Phil 3:18).

St Ignatius the God-bearer, in his Epistle to the holy martyr Polycarp, Bishop of Smyrna, says, "Take up all, as the Lord also has taken you up; carry all on your shoulders in charity … Bear the weaknesses of all, as a perfect athlete. Where there is the greater labor, there also shall be the greater reward. If you love good disciples, you have no thanks; strive rather to subdue with meekness those who are obstinate. Not every wound is healed by the same medicine; mollify those who are angry by pouring in oil."

Chrysostom, in his twenty-eighth homily on 2 Corinthians, writes, "And I shall bewail many who have sinned already. Not merely those who 'have sinned,' but also those who 'have not repented.' Consider the goodness of the Apostle: when he knows no evil of himself, he weeps for the evil that is in others, and humbles himself for their sins, for this is the perfection of our teaching, thus to sympathize with the ills of our disciples and thus to weep and mourn over the wounds of our hearers." The same Father in his forty-fourth homily on Acts, commenting on the following passage: "Watch, and remember, that for three years I did not cease to warn everyone night and day with tears" (Acts 20:31), and in other homilies on the Epistles reveals this pastoral duty in its fullness.

The priest should never cease to admonish sinners, as long as they never cease to sin, for the true physician never leaves the sick, as long as there is any hope, however small, of life. And we should never despair of the salvation even of those who lead the worst lives, since God has His own particular hours for calling us to faith or to repentance. Some He calls very early; others at the third hour; others at the sixth; or the ninth. He has mercy even for those who have remained idle almost to the very evening, to the eleventh hour (Matt 20:1, 6). Therefore, we should also follow the example of the apostles and though we may have "toiled all night and caught nothing," yet again, we "let down" our teacher's nets at the word of the Lord (Luke 5:5).

Chrysostom's sixth moral on 1 Timothy has the following: "We have already spoken largely to you of this, and will not cease to speak, unless indeed there is something better, unless you show yourselves amended." And further on in the same discourse, he says, "If you do not want us to be burdensome and grievous to you, act! Show that our work is finished; otherwise, we shall never cease to speak to you of the same things."

The fourth kind of teaching is this—the priest must guide the faithful in holy living. In this work the pastor should first admonish and persuade his people that "faith without works is dead" (James 2:20) and no more pleasing to God than a putrid corpse, and that is the reason that they who, like Hymenaeus and Alexander, have rejected a good conscience (1 Tim 1:19–20) openly fall away from the faith. At the same time, he should explain to them what true Christian virtue is and how far removed it is not only from hypocritical but also from philosophical or civil virtue, which seeks not God's glory but its own advantage. Also, he must explain that the Christian virtues, since they spring from one root—the love of God—are all so closely interwoven together that he who transgresses even against one of them becomes guilty of transgressing against all of them (James 2:10). Lastly, he should imprint it deeply on their hearts that the way to heaven is narrow, and the gate that leads to everlasting life is difficult (Matt 7:13–14).

Of course, instruction itself is useless if a priest does not practice what he preaches. A member of the clergy can and must reveal true godliness in his own life. He must make the striving for holiness comprehensible and vital for his parishioners. But first and foremost, he must reveal it to himself; he must live it, constantly being spiritually renewed and deepening his knowledge of the Church. A priest who is spiritually dead will not accept these words; they are not necessary to an ambitious seeker of awards and honors. But for the true pastor they are necessary, for his service is called to be fruitful and salvific both for him and for a multitude of our excellent children of the Church.

Furthermore, a priest must not "play a part," behaving himself differently in various situations; he must be himself everywhere. Every bit of affected unctuousness, every false tone will be perceived with disgust by those around him. Prayer, repentance, self-castigation, a desire for spiritual growth and for salvation—all is born from love for Christ. Love for mankind is a reflection, a direct consequence of love for the Son of God, Who was crucified and buried for our sake.

The fifth and last kind of teaching is to comfort the afflicted. Some afflictions are spiritual, others bodily. Among those who are spiritually afflicted, some weep for their transgressions (Matt 5:4), and not infrequently, from a sense of the enormity of their sinfulness, they despair of God's mercy (2 Cor 2:7–8). Others live religiously, but suffer temptations of the flesh (1 Pet 2:11), the world (1 John 2:15), and the devil (1 Pet. 5:8–9). Bodily afflictions, on the other hand, are either universal—such as famine, war, and pestilence—or else they are particular to the faithful—such as persecution for the faith (1 Pet 1:6–7; 3:14). In all these forms of affliction, the skillful pastor must give consolation abundantly from the word of God as from an ever-flowing fountain (2 Cor 1:4–5), but if he were to give consolation to unrepentant sinners, it would not heal them, but turn to their greater harm, for they require sharp, not mild, remedies, reproof, rather than consolation.

If the priest has to comfort any who suffer for righteousness' sake, especially for our holy faith, he should caution them, as Christians and good people, to do all they can to avoid persecution, to walk blamelessly in all things. "For this is commendable, if because of conscience toward God one endures grief, suffering wrongfully. For what credit is it if, when you are beaten for your faults, you take it patiently? But

if when you do good and suffer, if you take it patiently, this is commendable before God" (1 Pet 2:19–20). Christians who thus suffer have
fellowship in Christ's sufferings and glorify God (1 Peter 4:16).

As for those who are tempted by lust (James 1:13–14), the priest
should bear in mind that it is not only comfort that they need but also
admonition, lest they make light of their evil habits. He must help
them humble themselves before God, crying out with the apostle, "O
wretched man that I am! Who will deliver me from the body of this
death?" (Rom 7:24). He must help them strive with all their might to
mortify within themselves that lust that breeds their temptations in
its very conception (Col 3:5) lest, having "conceived, it gives birth to
sin; and sin, when it is full-grown, brings forth death" (James 1:15).

Lustful desires are no small evil. Apostle Peter commands us to
"abstain from fleshly lusts, because they war against the soul" (1 Pet
2:11), while in the Gospel our Lord Jesus Christ said, "these evil things
come from within and defile the man" (Mark 7:23). The tenth commandment also forbids every unjust wish of the heart and every hurt-
ful lust. "You shall not covet your neighbor's wife … " and so on (Exod
20:17). Therefore, everyone must pay attention and carefully reject all
lustful thoughts and desires, as it is written: "Beware lest there be a
hidden thought in your heart, a transgression of the law" (Deut 15:9).

Since the sole Author and Finisher of our holy faith, our everlasting salvation, is our Lord Jesus Christ (Heb 12:2), "there is no other
name under heaven given among men by which we must be saved"
(Acts 4:12) but only His; since "to Him all the prophets witness that,
through His name, whoever believes in Him will receive remission
of sins" (Acts 10:43) "and repentance and remission of sins should be
preached in His name" (Luke 24:47), it is plain that the priest must
instill the knowledge of Christ Jesus, inculcate His doctrine, dwell
on His exceeding compassion, and inspire the soul with the truth that
Christ "became for us wisdom from God—and righteousness, sanctification, and redemption" (1 Cor 1:30).

To the truth here stated—the foundation of all truth—we are led
by our Saviour Himself, when He says, "This is eternal life, that they
may know You, the only true God, and Jesus Christ Whom You have

sent" (John 17:3). Therefore Paul, for himself and the other Apostles, said the following: "We preach Christ crucified ... the power of God, and the wisdom of God" (1 Cor 1:23–24). And in another place, "Him we preach warning every man, and teaching every man in all wisdom, that we may present every man perfect in Christ Jesus" (Col 1:28). Following this doctrine and the example of the Apostles, every pastor of the Church, every preacher of the Word of God, in every kind or branch of teaching, whether he teaches faith, or holy living, whether he corrects the sinner, comforts the afflicted, or raises the fallen, must instill in his parishioners that Christ is the Son of God, the Light of the world, and that all who follow Him will not walk in darkness. He is the Good Shepherd, who lays down His life for the sheep (John 10:15); He is "the Lamb of God who takes away the sins of the world" (John 1:29); He is "the way, the truth, and the life" (John 14:6); He is the Door, the Resurrection, the awful Judge; He will "render to each one according to his deeds" (Rom 2:6), while "in flaming fire taking vengeance on those who do not know God, and on those who do not obey the gospel of our Lord Jesus Christ" (2 Thess 1:8). Depending on the circumstances, the priest can implant—and it is his duty to implant—the knowledge of Christ Jesus. Therefore, all instruction must be grounded in Christ, for all that can be either written or said with reference to the faith and everlasting happiness, if it is not grounded in faith in Christ, is unfruitful and can never save.

As for where and when it is the priest's duty to teach, priests should not think the church is the only place—or Sundays and Feasts the only times—for teaching. Following the example of the Apostle Paul, they must teach both in the church *publicly* and from *house to house* (Acts 20:20) all in common, and every one in particular, *day and night* (Acts 20:31), *in season and out of season*[19] (2 Tim 4:2). Priests must, when they visit the houses of their parishioners, duly examine whether they live godly lives, whether each fulfills the duties of his or her calling—husbands and wives theirs, parents theirs, children theirs, employers and employees theirs—and if it seems that they are not, then the priest should do his best to correct them, in whatever way is needed. Such visits, even if they are often repeated, will not offend the people, as long as they feel that their priest comes to them not for drink or presents but only to seek their salvation, as is his duty. This is absolutely required from the priest by his pastoral duty. For he is bound not to let one sheep be lost (Luke 15:4), even if he has the ninety-nine in safety. He must pay for the one that is lost by his negligence with his own soul; he must truly look after each one of his parishioners, watch the state of each, and know exactly, as though it were written on the palm of his hand, whether each abides by God's grace in health or is diseased with sin. He must recognize the particular sin, the danger of the disease, and what particular remedy is required. All this the priest cannot do without close inspection and knowledge of their lives, nor without going about among them and administering to each a suitable admonition, for there is no one common remedy for all diseases. The skillful physician who sees many different kinds of diseases examines their symptoms and only then prescribes particular remedies for each.

Thus, St John Chrysostom, in his thirty-fourth homily on Hebrews, has the following words: "For all who are entrusted to your care—men, women, and children—you, O Priest, will give account." The same Father, in his tenth homily on Matthew, writes thus: "As the careful householder knows what each person in his house needs, so should the priest know the morals, actions, and conversation of all, that he may be able to give medicine suitable to each; that he may comfort those who need comfort; and that he may rebuke those who need rebuke."

In order to properly admonish his parishioners, on whatever occasions he may be present—at commemorations, anointing, visiting the sick, the confession and communion of the dying, and other like occasions—the careful priest will not fail to offer such instruction and discourse as is suitable for the occasion, profiting both the sick and the rest who are present. By doing this, he turns the house itself into a church and gives spiritual food to the sick and others present. If he does this, he will not be found in the number of those miserable pastors, at whom the Apostle Jude seems to be pointing his finger, as he wrote, "These are spots in your love feasts, while they feast with you without fear, serving only themselves. They are clouds without water, carried about by the winds; late autumn trees without fruit" (Jude 1: 12).

So great is this work of teaching, not only in church but also from house to house, not only in season but also out of season, not only at set times, with preparation, but also at any moment, and offhand, that we cannot fail to see how necessary it is for the priest to be rich both in word and in wisdom to fulfill this great duty. The only way to ensure this is that he be skilled and nourished, if possible from childhood, in Holy Scripture (1 Tim 4:6).

From what has been said in the preceding sections of the absolute necessity of learning for the priesthood, it should be obvious that every priest and deacon, even every aspirant to the priesthood, should without fail—so far as time and strength permit—apply their whole souls to the study of Holy Scripture, and to understand it correctly, they should call upon the Lord as did David: "Give me understanding, and I shall delve into Thy law" (Ps 118:34 LXX). "Open Thou mine eyes, that I may recognize the wonderous things of Thy law" (Ps 118:18 LXX). At the same time, they should not neglect to study writings of the Holy Fathers, the Canons, and ecclesiastical history but should duly apply themselves to these studies and collect from them various examples and precedents, apt analogies and illustrations, and other knowledge to help them fulfill the duties of their calling. But if anyone is not disposed or not able to do this, then neither should he aspire to be a priest.

To study must become one of the clergyman's primary goals in life. The process of delving ever deeper into the established catechetical truths must never cease in him. The Gospel, the Bible—they cannot be read enough. One needs to read them throughout life, daily, living by what is written inside of them, for these are not worldly books of men but the words of life and salvation. Hence, a clergyman must treat the Bible and especially the New Testament and its pastoral passages in a very special manner. The Holy Gospel is always before the eyes of a priest—in the church and at home; it accompanies him even to the grave. He is the primary practitioner of the Gospel; he will answer to God for this. He is a teacher in word and life.

The Lord Himself commands that a pastor of the Church should be learned in the divinely inspired Scripture, and keep the word of God always in his mind, when he spoke thus: "Only take heed to yourself and diligently guard your soul, lest you forget all the things your eyes saw, and lest they depart from your heart all the days of your life; and you shall teach them to your sons and the sons of your sons" (Deut 4:9). And again: "This book of this law shall not depart from your mouth, and you shall meditate in it day and night, that you may have the understanding to do all things written therein. For then you will both prosper, make your ways prosperous, and have understanding" (Josh 1:8).

The Apostle Paul urges the same: "Give attention to reading, to exhortation, to doctrine … meditate on these things; give yourself entirely to them … " (1 Tim 4:13, 15). "Let the word of Christ dwell in you richly in all wisdom" (Col 3:16).

St Jerome, in his sixth moral on Leviticus VIII, has the following:

> If any one will be a priest not in name only, but in deed, let him imitate Moses; let him imitate Aaron. For what is written of these? "They departed not," saith the Scripture, "from the Tabernacle of the Lord," for Moses was continually in the Tabernacle of the Lord. But what need had he to be there? Either that he might himself learn something from God, or else that he might teach something to His people. These are the priest's two duties: the first, to learn himself from God by reading the Divine Scriptures, and hourly meditating on them; the second, to teach his people what he has himself learned from God, not of his own will, nor of the reason of man, but as the Holy Spirit teaches.

The Lord, through the Prophet Hosea, rejects from the priesthood the careless priest, even threatening his whole house: "Because you have rejected knowledge [that is, the doctrine of the Lord], I will also reject you from being priest for Me; and because you have forgotten the law of your God, I also will forget your children" (Hosea 4:6).

The apostle forbade those ignorant in the law and those who live disordered lives to be ordained to the priesthood, allowing only those who are able to teach others and live a blameless life. "And the thing that you have heard from me among many witnesses, commit these to faithful men who will be able to teach others also" (2 Tim 2:2). The second canon of the Seventh Ecumenical Council has these words: "Whoever would be a Bishop (the same applies to a priest) must be able to explain the Psalter, and understand all that he reads, and more than that, must have studied it, the sacred Canons, the Holy Gospel, the books of the Apostles, and all Divine Scripture: otherwise, let him not be ordained."

St John Chrysostom, in his fourth book *On the Priesthood*, writes of this at large and forcefully exhorts the priest: "that he fail not, as being the pastor of the Church, to give himself to the study of Divine Scripture, and become not only proficient in that study, but also in other sciences," and in support of this he gives weighty reasons. On the other hand, if anyone is careless and unlikely to know how to establish men in the holy faith by the word of God, or to guide them to repentance, he should not be ordained, says St John in the same discourse, for such a priest does great harm to his parishioners and will himself certainly fall under God's judgment. Here the priest should remember the parables of the evil husbandmen and the talents, as well as the parable of the Good Shepherd (John 10).

In conclusion, as a pattern of that instruction that the priest owes his people by word, we will offer the teaching of St Paul and his care for souls, in which, as in a pure mirror, nearly all our foregoing exhortations are clearly reflected. Let us look only at the twentieth chapter of the Acts of the Apostles.

1. What did St Paul teach? Does he merely repeat to his disciples the Lord's Prayer and that mechanically? No, how far was he from such unprofitable and careless teaching! He "kept back nothing that was helpful" (Acts 20:20). He testified "to Jews and also to Greeks, repentance toward God and faith toward our Lord Jesus Christ" (Acts 20:21). He did not shun "to declare to [them] the whole counsel of God" for their salvation (Acts 20:27).

2. Where did he teach? Was it in churches only and assemblies? By no means: not only before the people but also *from house to house* (Acts 20:20), not only all *publicly,* in their assembly, but also *everyone* of them in particular, by himself (Acts 20:31).

3. When did he teach? On Sundays and feast days only? Or only during Lent? No, he taught *day and night, for three years,* when he abode at Ephesus (20:31) *from the first day that [he] came to Asia,* during the whole time of his stay (Acts 20:18).

4. How did he teach? Was it harshly and with contention? By no means. He taught "with all humility, with many tears" (Acts 20:19).

5. To what end did he teach? Maybe for his own glory and honor? Not at all! He took no care whatever for himself, "nor [did he] count [his] life dear to [himself]," but he labored only "so that [he] may finish [his] race with joy, and the ministry which [he] received from the Lord Jesus, to testify to the gospel of the grace of God" (Acts 20:24).

6. Under what circumstances did he preach? Was he favored by opportunity and ease? Far from it: he was hindered by many trials and dangers, "by the plotting of the Jews" (Acts 20:19).

7. Lastly, had he any profit, however small, by his labors? Did he receive payment even for his necessary food and clothing? No! Even this most appropriate and reasonable tribute he would not accept. "I have coveted no one's silver or gold or apparel" (Acts 20:33). "These hands have provided for my necessities, and for those who were with me," while he preached the Gospel by both day and night (Acts 20:34). And this was the reason that the same great teacher could so boldly say, "Therefore I testify to you this day that I am innocent of the blood of all men" (Acts 20:26).

CHAPTER 4

On Instruction by Deed

The words of the teacher are so closely connected with his life and actions that even heathen rhetoricians have laid it down for a rule that no one can be a good orator unless he is first a good man. For they knew that if the teacher of virtue does not himself practice virtue, he gains no credit with his hearers. For they, seeing him doing one thing but saying another, think that he praises virtue for some personal gain, not because virtue deserves praise in itself, otherwise he would himself practice it. Therefore, he who lives sinfully while preaching virtue can never speak out boldly, lest his own conscience begin to rail at him: "Physician, heal yourself!" (Luke 4:23). Christ Himself says, "Hypocrite! First remove the plank from your own eye, and then you will see clearly to remove the speck from your brother's eye" (Matt 7:5). "Why dost thou preach My statutes, and takest My covenant in thy mouth?" (Ps 49:16). On the contrary, when the life of a preacher corresponds with his preaching, he can preach boldly, being ready to say to every man in the words of Christ, "Which of you convicts me of sin?" (John 8:46).

What qualities are required of a clergyman? Primarily reverence, as an expression of a deep-rooted fear of God, a recognition of the greatness of the work and the holiness of the place, and at the same time an awareness of one's unworthiness, weakness, sinfulness, and a whole-hearted trust in the love and mercy of God, a complete dedication and giving of oneself to God and neighbor. The ability to focus all the powers of one's soul and mind on the service, on its content and spiritual meaning, is also necessary. Here everything that is distracting or diverting your attention, everything irritating, all memories, all habits and cares must be cut off. And in general, inner discipline, composure, and restraint are always essential to a clergyman. Bearing witness to the faith of Christ—this is what the life of a clergyman should be. The most effective teaching, the most convincing form of apologetics is a worthy pastor who lives in profound faith in God and love for man, who is steeped in knowledge and culture, who is dedicated and principled. Interacting with people is a difficult business. Serving for the salvation of all people is a task of the utmost difficulty, unthinkable without prayer and help from God, impossible without the Church. The experience of the Church and, above all, the grace acting in the Church give the pastor great strength if he himself strives to put the commandments of our Lord Jesus Christ and all the institutions of the Church into practice in his life and service. Obedience to the Church, love for the Church, and a complete giving of oneself to the work of the priesthood—here is what makes a pastor always a pastor, both in the church and outside of it. A clergyman, by the very nature of his service, is called to be a spiritually sensitive person. A clergyman must combine his knowledge of people, human relations, human weaknesses and problems with a clear idea of the norms of human society and act boldly on that knowledge.

St John Chrysostom, in his fifth homily on 2 Thessalonian, says, "Great must be the teacher's boldness when he can instruct his disciples from his own good deeds, as Paul, when he said, 'For ye yourselves know that it is fit for you to be like unto us,' and in truth he should teach much more by life than by word."

If even heathen oratory required from its professors a good life, how much more must a preacher of the Gospel live virtuously, for which reason Christ when He sent the Apostles to preach called them the light of the world and at the same time explained what this light should be: "Let your light so shine before men, that they may see your good works and glorify your Father in heaven" (Matt 5:16), and a little further on, "Whoever does and teaches them, he shall be called great in the kingdom of heaven" (Matt 5:19). And He Himself describing the marks of a good pastor among the rest establishes the following:

"when he brings out his own sheep, he goes before them; and the sheep follow him, for they know his voice" (John 10:4). That is, it is not enough for a good Shepherd to call to his sheep with his voice alone, but he must also lead them by the example of his virtuous life, so that the sheep may follow in his track.

As Christ did to the Apostles, so the Apostles left this rule to their successors, the bishops and priests. Peter their chief, when he entreats the priests to shepherd the flock of God, at the same time points out how to feed it, "serving as overseers, not by compulsion, … but being examples to the flock" (1 Pet 5:2–3). And Paul, that other chief, teaches his disciple Timothy the same, saying, "be an example to the believers in word, in conduct, in love, in spirit, in faith, in purity" (1 Tim 4:12). To Titus he also said, "In all things showing yourself to be a pattern of good works, in doctrine showing integrity, reverence, incorruptibility, sound speech that cannot be condemned" (Titus 2:7–8).

All they who have left us this rule for teachers to live a holy life have also confirmed it by their own example. Of our Lord Jesus Christ Himself, St Luke at the beginning of the Acts of the Apostles chapter 1, verse 1, has these words: "Jesus began to do, and teach." Of John the Baptist Christ Himself bare witness saying, "He was the burning and shining lamp" (John 5:35). Paul dares to speak of himself thus: "Therefore I run thus: not with uncertainty. Thus I fight: not as one who beats the air. But I discipline my body and bring it into subjection, lest, when I have preached to others, I myself should become disqualified" (1 Cor 9:26–27). Therefore, since he conformed himself to Christ and followed Him in all things, he exhorted his disciples to do the same, saying, "Imitate me, just as I also imitate Christ" (1 Cor 11:1). Be followers of Paul, as he is of Christ: "Brethren, join in following my example, and note those who so walk, as you have us for a pattern" (Phil 3:17).

Clement of Alexandria, in his first *Stroma*,[20] says, "He is a true priest of the Church, and a true minister of the will of God, who both does and teaches what is of God." St John of Damascus, in his *Parallels*, quotes the following words from Didymus of Alexandria: "Then, at length, the teacher does his work, and his hearers believe him, when he teaches by his life and his deeds. As it is written, 'Jesus began to do and to teach.'"

From what has been said above anyone can see that a priest's life should be as similar as one hand is to the other, seconding and enforcing all he says for the edification of his people. St John Chrysostom, in his first homily on Acts, writes the following: "See how Christ gave His words force by His actions? This also He bade His disciples to do. For this reason, Paul also said, 'as you have us for a pattern,' (Phil 3:17) for nothing is more off-putting than a teacher who only philosophizes in words, for this shows not a teacher, but a hypocrite. Therefore, the apostles also taught first by life, and afterwards by word." Again, in his fifth homily on 1 Timothy, he writes, "The teacher should first teach himself; lest while he teaches others, he himself becomes a pariah. But let him have faith and a good conscience, and then let him teach others." Again, in his tenth homily: "The master should shine brighter than every light and have his life without a spot, so that all will look at him and conform their lives to his." Again, in his thirteenth homily: "Be a pattern to believers, that is, to your parishioners, in word, in life, in conversation, in charity, in faith, in purity, showing yourself to all as an example of good works. In other words, be yourself a pattern of life; stand as a model, as a living, breathing law, as a rule and handbook of good living. For this is the kind of teacher a priest should be."

Therefore, you who are a priest must pay attention to yourself and strive to lead a life in emulation of Christ, so that you will be able to say with St Paul "Imitate me," as I have also imitated Christ. But if your life will not agree with your own preaching of the Gospel, then your instructions, even if they profit the people, will be to yourself only for the greater condemnation. In actual fact, teaching with words alone is for the most part not only cold and powerless, as has been said above, but, what is more, even positively corrupting, for it breeds in many a suspicion that faith is no more than a fable and virtue only a pretext for covetousness, and so instead of causing the name of God to be glorified, it becomes dishonored: "You, therefore, who teach another, do you not teach yourself? You who preach that a man should not steal, do you steal? You who say, 'Do not commit adultery,' do you commit adultery? You who abhor idols, do you rob temples? You who make your boast in the law, do you dishonor God through breaking the law? For 'the name of God is blasphemed among the Gentiles because of you,' as it is written" (Rom 2:21–24). Therefore, the Lord threatens such teachers, saying, "Why dost thou preach My statutes, and takest My covenant in thy mouth?" (Ps 49:16).

Chrysostom, in his seventy-second sermon on Matthew, says, "What can be more wretched than a teacher who goes before his disciples and leads them with a life worthy of contempt, not vigilance? For every one who breaks the law is worthy of condemnation, but much more worthy of double and triple condemnation is he who is honored with the calling of teacher. First, because he transgresses; second, because, when he ought to amend others by his life, he corrupts them, deserving so much the heavier punishment in proportion to his greater honors and responsibilities; thirdly, because the teacher does the greater mischief, because he sins not simply as others, but also against his own teaching."

Also, in his sixth sermon on Romans, Chrysostom says, "The hearing of the law profits nothing, unless the doing of it follows. Nor is this true of hearing only, but of teaching also, which is more than hearing. Nor will it be any excuse for the teacher, if he does not do himself that which he teaches to others, but rather it will result in his greater punishment." And further on, in the same sermon, he says, "What profit is there in teaching, if you do not teach yourselves, not yourselves only, but others also, to do what is proper? Or, what is far crueler, if you not only neglect to teach the things of the Law, but even teach what is contrary?" The whole sermon speaks of the same issue.

Furthermore, the same Father, in his thirtieth moral on Acts, has the following words:

Why are you proud that you teach with words? But it is easy to philosophize in words. Teach me by your life: that is teaching indeed! You say that it is right to be humble, and give a long discourse about this, without being ever at a loss for words, but whoever teaches me with his actions is a better preacher than you. Teaching by words does not fall so deep into the soul as teaching by deeds, for without deeds, not only do your words bring no profit, but rather they do harm. It is better to be silent. Why? Because you are commending to me a thing impossible, for I think that if you, who says all this, does not do it, of course I can be excused, since I say nothing of the kind. For this reason, the Prophet says, 'But unto the sinners God said, Why dost thou preach My statutes?' (Psalm 49:16) for this is all the more harm, if any one teaching in words, overthrows his own doctrine with his deeds. This it what makes many in our churches lead evil lives.

St Jerome, in his second epistle to Nepotianus, says, "See that your life does not hinder your words. When you teach in the Church, give no one any reason to say to you, even in secret, 'Why do you not do that what you teach? You are an admirable teacher, who, while eating and drinking, teaches temperance! At this rate a robber may denounce stealing!' Christ's priest should have his lips, his heart, and his deeds all in agreement."

St John of Damascus, in his treatise on icons, has the following passage: "Either teach not at all, or teach by your life, lest, while you invite men with your words, you drive them away with your actions."

Turning to the Scriptures, we see God Himself, through the mouth of His apostle, give a characterization of a proper clergyman: "A Bishop [or any clergyman] must be blameless, the husband of one wife, temperate, sober-minded, of good behavior, hospitable, able to teach; 3 not [a]given to wine, not violent, [b]not greedy for money, but gentle, not quarrelsome, not [c]covetous; 4 one who rules his own house well, having his children in submission with all reverence 5 (for if a man does not know how to rule his own house, how will he take care of the church of God?); 6 not a [d]novice, lest being puffed up with pride he fall into the same condemnation as the devil." On this subject St Paul also treats at length in the first chapter of Titus verses 6 through 9.

BLAMELESS: The first thing that the Holy Spirit—through the mouth of the Apostle Paul—requires is that the bishop or priest be blameless. In other words, as this word implies, he must be guiltless of any vice or any deed of a disgraceful nature, especially everything beyond natural infirmities, including murder, adultery, robbery, and the like. Also, he must be free from those other vices that the apostle lists, and not only this, he must also exercise all the virtues. To this directly refers what the apostle writes to Titus (1:8): "A Bishop [as well as a priest] must be … just and holy." Both these words, like "blameless," signify virtue in general, as well as all the particular virtues separately, especially all that are appropriate for a teacher and pastor of the Church.

THE HUSBAND OF ONE WIFE: The priest must be the husband of one wife. According to the interpretation of St John Chrysostom, Apostle Paul does not say this as laying down a law that there could be no unmarried priests, but in the sense that if married, he must not marry again after the death of his wife. This way of understanding the apostle's words is not only confirmed by the canons, and the interpretation of many of the Fathers, but is sufficiently clear from the fifth chapter of the same Epistle, for the apostle, requiring the widow to be, in like manner, *the wife of one husband*, plainly distinguishes her from those widows, who, after the death of their husbands, *marry again*.

This virtue is therefore prescribed to the priest to protect him from giving way to sensual pleasures or other weaknesses, which would bring dishonor and reproach on the priesthood himself. Therefore, the first canon of the Council of Neo-Caesarea orders that if a priest, because of the temptation to give way to sensual pleasures, chooses to marry, he must leave the priesthood, but if he commits fornication, he is to be excommunicated. "Let the Priest who marries cease from his ministry: but if he commit fornication, or adultery, let him be ousted, and placed among the penitents."

VIGILANT: St John Chrysostom understands this word to mean vigilance of soul in particular, that is, unceasing watchfulness over the flock entrusted to him. But neither does this word exclude bodily vigilance or sobriety, since this greatly assists the former, and the spiritual cannot exist without the bodily. Our Saviour Himself, when He exhorts us to watch for His coming, joins together both kinds of vigilance: "But take heed to yourselves, lest your hearts be weighed down with carousing, drunkenness ... Watch therefore, and pray always" (Luke 21:34, 36). The Apostle Peter, arming us against our adversary the devil, joins together sobriety and vigilance (1 Pet 5:8).

SOBER-MINDED, σώφρονα:[21] This word denotes a man who has the knowledge and power to bridle all his passions, especially carnal lust. Therefore, the word *sobriety* in this sense often means purity, and such purity is revealed not only in deeds but also in the thoughts that proceed out of the heart (for "out of the heart proceed ... adulteries," and so on "these are the things which defile a man" (Matt 15:19–20)). This sobriety also applies to the eyes, lips, and all the senses and movements of the body. Similar to this is the word *temperate*, for if a man is temperate in eating and drinking, such temperance is a part of sobriety, but if we take the word in a wider sense, it applies not only to eating and drinking but to all desires and passions of the flesh. Therefore, *temperate* in this wider sense means the same thing as *sober*.

Augustine says, "Do not say that you have pure hearts if you do not also have pure eyes, for an impure eye is the herald of an impure heart." St John Chrysostom, in his third book on the priesthood, has these words: "The priest ought to be as pure as if he stood in heaven itself, surrounded by the heavenly powers." The same Father, in his second moral on Titus, writes thus: "It is not the man who fasts that is here spoken of by the Apostle, but the man who subdues all his passions—those of the tongue, the hands, the wanton eyes. For this is temperance: to give in to no vice."

It must be mentioned that the passions opposed to sobriety or temperance—such as fornication or adultery—are so deadly and foul that they are utterly incompatible with the priesthood. There-fore, according to the canons of the holy Fathers,[22] not only is the priest guilty of these sins judged unworthy of the priesthood, but if a wife falls into such sins, it is an impediment to his priesthood, even if he is already ordained.[23] In order to prevent even a suspicion of such evil, the canons forbid priests and deacons who have been widowed to house any women except a mother, sister, aunt, or another close female relative.[24]

DEVOUT: The apostle speaks of *devotion* and *godly fear* in the same breath: "Let us have grace, by which we may serve God acceptably with reverence and godly fear" (Heb 12:28). Also we read of Cornelius, "a devout man, and one who feared God with all his household, who gave alms generously to the people, and prayed to God always" (Acts 10:2). Therefore, it is clear that a devout man is one who fears God and truly worships Him. This devotion is twofold: (1) inward and spiritual, when a man has devout faith, love, and fear of God, worshiping Him in spirit and in truth (John 4:24). (2) outward and bodily, which proceeds from the inward, when a man offers up prayers and thanksgiving to the Lord and worships Him with his body, when he hears or reads the word of God with pleasure and when he gives alms to the poor. This virtue, though required for every Christian, is for the priest no less necessary than the soul is for the body, especially when he stands before God's altar interceding for all and invoking the Holy Spirit to consummate the awesome Sacrifice. And if prayer is the priest's chief obligation, then it must not be restricted only to the services, to a definite rite or order. A pastor should be in prayer entirely and at all times. Prayer must not be assigned to certain times and days. He who does not pray at home will not be able to pray in church (on this subject, see Part III, where the priest's duty of prayer is treated at length).

OF GOOD BEHAVIOR: This expression denotes a man who observes the propriety that is appropriate for the priesthood in his actions, words, gait, dress, housekeeping, etc. A few detailed observations will be offered on this point.

First of all, a priest must be conscientious about his manner of serving in church. A priest's appearance and his serving style—meaningful, unhurried, but also not drawn out—clearly pronounced exclamations with emphasis on important phrases and dignified movements—all of this acts beneficially on the congregation. They see and feel that their priest's service is sincere, pious, without artifice, affectation, or false humility.

At the beginning of a service, while vesting, a priest reads special prayers as he blesses the vestments. He must also read another set of prayers while taking off the vestments. It is painful to see vestments being taken off carelessly and hastily or to see vestments lying in disarray inside the altar or vestry.

It is important for vestments always to be in order and correspond in color to the day and service, and also that all the parts of the vestments correspond to one another in color. For instance, one must not wear a green orarion with a blue sticharion or red cuffs with a blue phelonion, etc. Aesthetic taste is needed here. It is senseless to sew red ribbons onto a blue under-vestment. Incidentally, a priest looks very bad in an under-vestment that is too short. This should be avoided at all costs.

It is also important for the pastor to have command of his voice, to know the shortcomings of his pronunciation, diction, and pitch, and to persistently struggle with them. For this it is useful to listen carefully to constructive criticism and take it into consideration. Every speech defect inhibits pastoral work. Ostentation and affectation must also be cast aside. It is essential to help the congregation grasp clearly and distinctly everything said by the deacon or priest. Clamorous serving, as well as serving that is too quiet, harms pastoral work. Some young clergymen, in the early days of their service, imitate older priests' incorrect faulty habits of serving and giving exclamations. There is a significant danger here: having at a young age acquired erroneous serving habits, a priest can remain a captive of these mistakes until the end of his days.

Nevertheless, it is necessary that one learn from those who are experienced and live an active spiritual life. It is helpful to compare the practices of different clergyman and to read about this in more detail. The pastor should ask himself: Is there sense in this or that gesture, intonation, or movement? Are they justified? Do they aid in leading the flock to God, or is it personal arbitrariness, a cheap trick, poor style, or—worse yet—a show?

The sinful habit of rushing services results in muttering through one's nose, babbling, and the disappearance of words or even entire phrases. It is easy to become careless with diction, but this defect is difficult or even impossible to correct. There are old priests who are not able to serve due to this problem. A clergyman who is starting out should always remember this. Diction is an important element in reading. At home it is necessary to read aloud more expressively, to pay attention to one's articulation, and to listen to oneself carefully.

It is a bad thing for a priest to have a poor ear or a quiet voice, but even in such a situation there are ways of correcting the problem and improving, provided he is not overly proud or conceited and has the desire to improve. You often hear certain priests deliver exclamations in a repulsive manner, disfiguring the service. Deacons sometimes swell almost to bursting with pride, but actually, they are nothing to listen to: they serve atrociously, with a voice not their own. But just try to say something, give advice, or stop them! It is very difficult at times to hold back one's admonishments when a young priest is wailing, or meowing, or grunting, or mumbling the beginnings, or shouting as loud as two people together, or serving in a bass voice when he is actually a tenor. They often serve vulgarly, rudely, or in a soft, affected manner. These matters of pitch, voice, and diction are very, very important, and the priest must not rely solely on his own opinion of his qualities, considering the opinion of others as being always untrue and spiteful.

The outward appearance of a pastor is also not of minor importance. In this regard, our clergymen could probably be divided into those who are completely shaven with close-cropped hair, those who have beard and hair of moderate length, and those who are altogether unshaven and untrimmed. It seems to me that a priest should respect himself, his office, and the traditions of the Church, but that it is absolutely not mandatory that he grows his hair and beard down to his waist. Shaving one's neck, doing one's hair up into disgraceful braids in the manner of peasant priests, and long unkempt beards certainly do not add any "additional orthodoxy" to those who wear them. A priest's outward appearance should be well kept. Naturally, he should not style his beard to look like an artist or a dandy, but neither does he need to be a porcupine or a scarecrow. A beard and hairstyle that are moderate in length will always testify that a priest is not concealing himself and that he bears the dignity of his ordination with worthiness.

A priest's clerical garb must be simple. The best color for a riassa and podryasnik is always black. Of course, there may be variations but very moderate ones. Flashy riassas and podryasniks of different colors, or those made from expensive fabrics, often effeminate or shiny, or those made of velvet—all this does not speak in favor of their owners. A love of extremely wide, colorful belts also does not always indicate good taste. The shoes worn during services should be simple, black, and thoroughly cleaned. The priest is forbidden by the canons to wear fine gowns or to go in dirt and tatters, for the first in a priest shows softness or vanity, while the second is a mark of hypocrisy.[25]

The image of the priest in a riassa with a cross on his chest has been shaped through the centuries, and it should not be defaced. Shaven cheeks and stubble in place of a beard, a riassa that, for some reason, is in Greek style, yellow shoes—none of this enhances the appearance of a Russian Orthodox priest. A riassa, just like a podryasnik, should be our own—Russian. Monks of any rank should not wear colored podryasniks. They, more than anyone, need to keep modesty in mind. A priest should avoid, as much as possible, appearing in church in only a podryasnik, which is essentially the same as an undergarment. A black skufia is the best adornment for a clergyman.

It is impermissible to appear only in a podryasnik in official settings—in the presence of a bishop, in an ecclesiastical school, or in the ruling hierarch's residence. Here a priest must be dressed officially, wearing a pectoral cross. A monk, in these instances, should be in his klobuk and have his prayer rope. A riassa, when possible, should not be short, so that one's pants do not peep out from underneath: this is unsightly.

Occasionally—although this is extremely unfortunate and should be avoided if at all possible—a priest is compelled to wear secular clothing in public. It should be simple and in good taste. It is better to choose dark colors and clothes that are simple in design: a black suit, white shirt, black tie, black shoes, and a dark, modest overcoat and hat. Bright, stylish suits, hats, shoes, berets, crude open-collared and sleeveless shirts are inappropriate. Modesty always adorns a person and never degrades him. The ability to properly pick out and wear clothing is by no means given to everyone.

Priests greatly err when they try to become one of the crowd, to be like everyone else! It is painful to see a priest poorly "disguised" as a secular person. It is no coincidence that in folk wisdom it is said you can always tell a preacher, even if he is in rags. But it should not simply be a preacher who is seen, but a contemporary pastor. For a pastor is a person who is deeply cultured, a person who is spiritually and aesthetically rich. It is not being old-fashioned and having bad taste, nor is it being detached from the times one lives in, but rather, it is an awareness of the need and importance of pastoral work that should define the behavior and appearance of a priest of the Ortho-dox Church. A clergyman who wears his ecclesial attire with honor always evokes respect from those around him. Wicked is that miser-able priest, the rite-performer, who, when he has carelessly finished a service, hangs up his riassa, leaving with it everything pertaining to the priestly office until the next service and rushes out into the world, as does a person who is altogether secular and non-spiritual, thirsting for the pleasures and entertainments this world has to offer.

Even a clergyman's gait must be respectful. It is impermissible to run about the altar and church, wave one's hands or head, or toss one's hair; one must also not intentionally "float," barely moving one's feet. This is pretension. One's gait should be natural, but steady, so as not to disrupt the general dignity and harmony of the service. One must skillfully calculate one's entrances and exits, to neither rush nor be late. There should be no pauses during the services. The services must begin at a strictly appointed time. It is inexcusable to be late or to arbitrarily change the time for services.

It goes without saying that a clergyman must be clean. His face, hands, mouth, and his whole body must always be impeccably washed.

It is the duty of every altar-server to continually look after himself. A pastor's personal hygiene, neatness, and cleanliness must become an integral part of his life. It is sad to see a priest who is unkempt, with overgrown hair, blackened nails, and rotten teeth. Such a priest brings harm to this great work by his want of culture and shames the clergy as a whole.

Among the clergy there is no place for cologne, makeup, hair color, manicures, or curling one's hair. Things of this sort are incompatible with the character of a priest, and only people who are spiritually impoverished seek to decorate themselves in this fashion. It should also be obvious to anyone that it is not acceptable for clergymen to smoke. For the faithful, a priest or deacon smoking is an appalling sight.

There is another aspect of priestly life that is rarely discussed—the need for a priest to be a cultured man. We will dwell on the issue of a pastor's personal culture in more detail, since this issue is very important for a clergyman. The concept of personal culture is multifaceted. It is not only the outward appearance of a person, his speech, and behavior in society but mainly his inner spiritual wealth, his interests, his actual—not feigned—outward culture. There is no need to speak about the importance of an education for a clergyman—both of a general and of a particular nature—it should already be obvious. A spiritual education must be considered the norm for every clergyman. However, it is a bad seminary graduate or doctoral candidate of theology who does not continue his education after leaving the walls of his theological school. A school gives merely the key to future knowledge and further development. It is pleasant to see parish clergymen working on their chosen master's topics, not breaking off with theological studies, being interested in developing them, writing and reading. A priest who has sunk into simply being a formal performer of rites is a spiritual sluggard. But a priest who wastes himself on a passion for sports or entertains himself with secular reading is an absolutely repulsive phenomenon.

A clergyman's range of interests should be broad. Other than his main theological and ecclesiastical knowledge, he should be well versed in general knowledge, in the discoveries and achievements of the secular sciences. Each person naturally inclines toward this or that area of learning. It is good when a clergyman's range of interests covers those disciplines that help him to better and more fully perform his pastoral service. The study of history, literature, the arts, logic, philosophy, psychology, music, languages, and other spheres of learning can be very beneficial to a pastor.

A clergyman can supplement and broaden his knowledge through self-education. There are many ways of educating oneself—it all depends on the desire and ability to organize one's time, on the ability to delve into a book and to think constructively. Intelligent reading, note-taking, critical evaluation of what has been read—all of these are important components in the process of self-education.

Self-education should be a systematic, consistent, continuous process, not merely occasional reading. It is very beneficial for a clergyman to study the history of the Church, general history, and to be familiar with the leading literature on these topics. Old theological periodicals, diocesan journals, and the like are rich in material. A knowledge of the history and life of eminent spiritual figures, along with their works and their writings, greatly adds to a clergyman's "toolbox" and helps him in his service.

As we said before, books must be a pastor's constant companions. The clergyman's personal library should be compiled lovingly and thoughtfully, taking into consideration the needs of the pastor, as well as his spiritual children—this is his irreplaceable treasure! It is difficult in general to acquire a library, especially a pastoral one, but it can and should be done. It is important for this library to include reference books, encyclopedias, concordances, dictionaries, manuals, and other such books. Every kind of collecting contains in itself the danger of its growing into a passion, but a priest must collect spiritual books; they will impart much to the pastor who reads and reflects on his reading. A love of books is one of the most significant indicators of real culture. Ancient hand-written manuscripts, early editions, or other rare and valuable books should find in the clergyman an unparalleled friend and careful guardian.

The ability to work with a book includes working with a pen. Copying out excerpts from one's reading, recording sermons, keeping a pastoral diary, notes from the services throughout the year, questions for clarification, jotting down unknown terms and words, official and personal correspondence—all of this requires a pastor's diligence to put his own thoughts to paper, as well as those of others. Reading and writing are connected with the spoken word, with homiletics, and with the culture of speech in general, about which more will be said below.

Written communication with people and correspondence, both official and personal, are an integral part of life. The ability to write briefly, clearly, and correctly should be developed starting from one's student years. Wordiness, ambiguity, mistakes, careless, ugly handwriting, the inability to correctly format an official document—these should be in every way eliminated.

A letter is a person's identity, his calling card. Business letters, social letters, congratulatory letters, and so forth should have their own character and be remarkable for their clarity of expression. Naturally, one's signature should contain one's full rank, name, surname (by no means using the word "father" in relation to oneself, just as in everyday speech), and the date. One must not write without a greeting, without leaving a signature (or by leaving a type-written signature); likewise, one must not send a printed copy of a letter—all of this suggests lack of culture. If a letter is sent with a person who is to be trusted, the envelope should not be sealed. There exists a practice of beginning a letter with the words "good day" or "hello"—this is atrocious. A private letter may begin as one pleases, as long as it contains a salutation. In official correspondence (memoranda, petitions, reports to superiors) the salutation in the document, as well as the rest of the document, should be composed in a professional manner.

It should be remembered that one must not write to the highest superiors "over the head" of one's immediate superior; this is a violation of the established order. One should always write to a bishop using his full title: "his grace, bishop so-and-so," indicating his diocese and fully identifying oneself as the priest of such-and-such a church, residing at such-and-such an address. It is customary to close these official letters in the following manner: "your grace's humble servant" priest, name, and surname (naturally, without flourish). An archimandrite is called "very reverend," just as archpriests are referred to now. Sometimes priests write "Christ is in our midst" at the beginning of letters. One may write only to clergy in this way. Among clergy it is also customary to draw a small cross at the top of letters. Correctness in letter writing is a very positive quality in a cultured person.

An interest in church antiquity, in its culture and history, should always dwell in the heart of the pastor. When visiting other churches, cities, and museums the priest should learn to look, compare, and discover to distinguish epochs, schools and styles of architecture, iconography, painting, and ecclesiastical ware. Books on history and art can be of invaluable service in this regard. It is a good thing for a priest to write a research project on church history or church archeology. A lively interest in the past is a good indicator of a pastor's genuine culture.

A clergyman should train himself to see the beauty of nature and works of art and antiquity. He must have a driving thirst for knowledge, a striving toward the beautiful, the sublime, and the spiritual. Beautiful music, the marvelous riches of literature—all must be accessible and important to an active, intelligent, sensible, and cultivated clergyman; everything must open up to him the wealth of God's world and everything must raise up his soul and reason to the Creator and Provider of all. Such wide-ranging possibilities for growth, such manifold paths to fascinating work, pursuits, and discoveries, will be found for every person, everyone who wishes and strives to learn more than he knows. Reading, traveling, discourse, reflection, and again reading—these are the basic milestones on this glorious journey.

A very important indicator of any person's culture is his manner of speech. Therefore, cultured speech is absolutely essential to a clergyman; he must learn to speak clearly, correctly, with literary language, allowing no rough or coarse language. The ability to listen to another person is likewise an essential quality in a clergyman. To hear a person out, to let him speak fully, is a great art. While doing this it is essential to listen, not interrupting, not brushing aside the other person's arguments, even if they do not correspond with one's personal views.

At this point it is proper to note that the canons of the Church and the precepts of the holy Fathers give some specific directions regarding personal appearance and behavior. Bishops and priests are forbidden to keep luxurious tables by Canon XV of the fourth Council of Carthage, which runs thus: "Let a Bishop have a humble establishment and table, and strive to maintain the dignity of his order by faith and holy living." The pagan historian Ammianus Marcellinus described the early Christian bishops in these words: "Some Bishops by their simple diet, their great temperance in drink, and their plain clothing, present themselves pure and honorable in the eyes of the eternal God and His true worshippers."

To act like a buffoon, to play cards, dance, or even to look at dancing is prohibited by the canons.[26] However, the expression "to play the buffoon" in these canons is somewhat obscure, and a few clarifications concerning this are in order.

To interfere in other people's conversations, to interrupt one's partners in discussion, and to make fun of them is rude and uncultured. One must not speak at the table when one's mouth is full with food. When socializing, the priest should not strive to have all those present listen only to him and agree only with him. He must not fasten himself to everyone, teach everyone, criticize, make jokes about those present, or make rude remarks. Rudeness in general should be absent in a clergyman's behavior. Harsh shouts, words, movements, and gestures do not grace anyone. Every kind of rudeness is a sign of extremely low, poor culture. Anger, touchiness, pettiness, and remembrance of wrongs are unfavorable qualities in any person and all the more so in a person invested with the dignity of the sacred office. A priest's word should be truthful and honest; when speaking, a pastor must always remember that he will give an answer to God for every one of his words, because improper behavior and offensive words from a priest can be a temptation for many. One should be careful with one's humor. Although an old seminary anecdote may be appropriate in the circle of one's former schoolmates, it may sound offensive and even shocking in different society.

Courtesy adorns every person and, along with modesty and tact, is an essential quality in a clergyman. It is also important to be able to begin a discussion, lead it, and develop interesting and edifying topics during conversation. Thoughtful conversation always shows the spiritual level of the one with whom you are conversing, his knowledge and interests. Moderate and intelligent humor, without bitterness or spite, enriches speech. At the same time, striving to be the "life of the party" or a comedian, spouting witticisms and anecdotes (usually not altogether new or refined), picking apart others behind their backs, gossiping and other such cankers of the soul—none of this should find a place in a clergyman.

The dignity and honor of ordination requires great care, both in the priest's choice of friends and companions and in his behavior with unfamiliar people. Intelligent, interesting conversation may do much, but the priest should always keep in mind the Gospel saying about the pearls and the swine. He should not start arguments and disputes about the faith with unknown people and in places that are altogether unsuitable for this. It is foolish at all times and everywhere to put himself forward his knowledge, merits, and acquaintances.

Although spiritual or parochial topics of conversation are understandable for those who are churchly, they may be altogether unclear and even harmful for those who are not churchly or only nominally interested in the Church. A priest's speech should be intelligent, tactful, and must not offend or disturb anyone nor lead anyone into despondency. The words of a pastor, both from the ambo and in personal conversation, should convey hope in God's love and His mercy.

The priest must not be shy of people or answer their questions dryly or even rudely. It is always necessary to speak the truth and to be sincere and honest with a person. It is very important for him to be exact, precise, and to know how to conduct himself in society. Assemblies of people can be different, but in whatever society a clergyman finds himself in, he must know how to be an Orthodox pastor above all. Not a mask but an honest and direct awareness of one's position, one's office, must be inherent in a pastor. It is easy to lose dignity or respect in the eyes of others; to earn true respect and authority, however, is not always easy.

A clergyman is called not to frighten people but to call them to rebirth, repentance, and salvation. Friendliness, warmth, simplicity, love, and approachability are the most essential qualities in a clergyman. Pride, arrogance, conceit, and pride in one's rank are always repulsive. Parochialism and taking stock of awards are a big problem for clergy.

Tactful behavior, politeness, and courtesy are integral qualities of a cultured person. One need not forget about such pleasant words as "allow me," "permit me," "please," "forgive me," "excuse me," and "would you be so kind." When in company, one must not sneeze loudly, blow one's nose, hiccup, cough loudly, or make a racket with chairs, doors, or dishes. Incidentally, it is improper for a clergyman to spit not only on the floor but also on the ground when outdoors.

Here we shall briefly touch on the issues concerning labor and health. Labor is an essential part of life. A hardworking clergyman is a good example for Christians. Industriousness always adorns a person. Every labor performed lovingly, honestly, and with care is praiseworthy. We need not be afraid of labor; we need not fear calluses. Labor is beneficial and wonderful for everyone! All of the great Christian ascetics were toilers and diligent workers. Idleness, laziness, and fear of work are unsightly traits that repulse people. And it is not only office and mental work but also physical work that is beneficial to every person in every respect. And woe to those who disdain work!

Work also saves one from sicknesses. Our health is a great gift from God and one must treat it with care and attention. Of course, one must not think only about oneself and one's health, talk about it continually, search out sicknesses and continually be under treatment, particularly since sickness can be imagined. However, if treatment is required, an illness should not be neglected; our health and well-being are important parts of our service and they must not be ignored. Consultation of a doctor in a timely fashion and a knowledge of one's own body are essential. Neglect of one's health is sinful.

In conclusion of this rather lengthy section, we repeat that it is unthinkable for a contemporary, intelligent clergyman to brush knowledge and culture aside; extensive knowledge, a high level of culture, a wide range of interests are essential for his life and work. Ignorant is the priest for whom culture and the arts do not exist, who considers any knowledge other than his own pastoral knowledge to be harmful. The Church's misfortune is that such ignorance, weakness, and spiritual poverty bring harm to the Church. An abundance of knowledge and true culture bring only benefit to the clergyman in his exalted service.

HOSPITABLE:[27] This is true of any house, but especially true that the house of a bishop or priest should be open to strangers. For how will the priest preach hospitality to others if he shuts his door to strangers? Nor should he be kind to strangers only, but also to all who need his help. He should be especially helpful to the poor and the sick, to take care of orphans, to defend widows and the oppressed, and to take the part of the innocent.[28] But if this seems impossible for poor priests, since they need assistance themselves, let them remember the apostles who worked with their own hands and still remembered the poor (Gal 2:10) and supported the weak (Acts 20:35). Moreover, following the example of the apostles, they should inspire those parishioners who have money to practice this virtue (1 Cor 16:1; 2 Cor 8:19).

St Jerome, in his second Epistle to Nepotian, says, "It is the glory of bishops to minister to the wants of the poor, and a disgrace for any priest to seek to enrich himself … If you have more than you need for your own food and clothing, give it away, knowing that you are bound to do this … He who leaves himself more than he needs is no better than a thief."

In a more general sense, a priest must also take care when visiting parishioners and inviting them to his own home. If he has come to a house, he must respect the hosts, their routines, their hospitality. He must not disdain bread and salt offered from a pure heart. But he needs to always remember what kind of house he is entering or whom he is bringing into his own house. There are many pits and dangers on this path!

Knowing how to conduct oneself in society, knowing how to sit, stand, change position—all of this is a matter of culture; all this can and should be done gracefully, lightly, without offending or jostling others.

A priest must not talk too loudly or address someone sitting far across the table; he must not point at anyone with his finger or fork, or wave his knife around during conversation. Forks, knives, and napkins must be used properly, naturally, without affected flourish. He must eat quietly and neatly, without stuffing his mouth with food.

Naturally, he must never rest his elbows on the table, jostle his companion, embrace him, or clap him on the shoulder. He must always take into consideration the place and character of a discussion and what sort of people are present. He should know when, with whom, and about what to speak. Knowing when to keep silent is a great art. To speak in such a way so that no one is hurt or offended, to speak interestingly and intelligently, is a matter of a person's tactfulness and abilities. Raucous laughter never graces a conversation. He who shouts with laughter excessively is foolish. An intentionally melancholy partner in conversation evokes confusion as well.

A priest should not request seconds at table, striving for moderation in food and especially in drink. Drinking is the single greatest danger for a clergyman. Feeding and entertaining the priest were always considered a matter of honor, and the priest did not want to offend any of his flock when visiting their homes. And what came of it? Unfortunately, it is no secret, there have been and still are clergymen who have a weakness for wine, a vice that will be discussed in greater detail.

It is helpful for a priest to watch how his elders behave at the table and to know the traditions unique to each home. Conversation during meals should not be about matters that spoil the mood or appetite. He should never make critical remarks about the food, the table settings, or the way the dishes are served—all of this is insulting to the hosts. He should not comment on mistakes made by the hosts or those sitting at the table. He should eat whatever is served and, of course, not speak about what the doctor has prohibited him to eat for health reasons.

A priest must not sit down or rise from the table before his elders. If he is the eldest, he should take his seat at the hosts' invitation and get up only once he has seen that everyone has eaten. It is good to bring the meal to a close with the hosts' consent. If the priest must leave early, let him excuse himself and leave, bidding everyone farewell with a general bow. He should take leave of the hosts separately. He should not allow them to wait on him excessively, help him into his coat, and so on. Self-service in such cases is always more preferable.

If the priest is hosting guests at his own home, he should greet them individually and, if they are not acquainted with one another, introduce them straightway. While doing this, he should give their full names. He should introduce the members of his own household as well. It is important that all the guests receive the hosts' attention and that the discussion be interesting to everyone. He should not call the guests to the table immediately; there should be conversation for a little while. The host must seat the guests himself.

He must entertain kindly, sometimes insistently, but without any force or pushiness, lest there be too much of a good thing. Special attention should be given to ladies and the elderly. The style of a reception is determined by its nature and by the guests. In the home of a priest, everything must be determined by his own style, which must not allow for extravagance, loud noise, inappropriate music, etc. The joy of friendship should by no means be expressed with tumultuous uproar.

Cultured behavior is always the same—whether at home or when visiting. But at home it requires still more skill and attentiveness from the host.

ABLE TO TEACH: "Holding fast the faithful word as he has been taught" (Titus 1:9). This quality of being *able to teach* is required of the priests, as St John Chrysostom also testifies in commenting on this passage, and this has been treated at length earlier in this book. Here it would be enough to mention what priests should do if—contrary to the apostolic command—they have been ordained without sufficient learning. For such priests, our preceding words concerning self-education and self-cultivation are especially appropriate. Specifically, to study books of the Holy Fathers, especially of St John Chrysostom, is absolutely indispensable. Priests should sometimes, whenever appropriate, read to the people a homily from St John Chrysostom.

In any case, the priest ought to have his life so clearly marked by true holiness that it will be a loud trumpet, able to awaken and incite all people to the fear of God, to devotion, and to imitation of his blameless and Christian life. Blessed Augustine, in the fourth book of his *On Christian Doctrine*, says: "If anyone is incapable of speaking either wisely, or eloquently, he can still let his life speak for itself, not only to gain a reward for himself, but also to give a pattern of emulation to others. Thus, his life will be a fitting replacement for an overabundance of words."

As we have already said above in detail, priests can also learn a great deal from sacred and ecclesiastical history, from sermons of contemporary preachers, from the lives of the Holy Fathers, as well as from other narratives that may encourage the reader to contemplate the working of God's Providence. All these will afford rich sources of instruction.

NOT GIVEN TO WINE: Among other vices that the apostle finds atrocious in a priest of the Church, he prominently features drunkenness. Of what countless other evils is this the cause! The daily suffering of alcoholics—and indeed one's own conscience—sufficiently shows this to be true. As for its foulness in God's sight, the word of God clearly witnesses to the seriousness of this vice. In the Old Testament drunkenness was forbidden to priests under pain of death: "Do not drink wine and strong drink, you nor your sons with you, when you go into the tabernacle of testimony, or when you approach the altar; lest you die. (it shall be an ordinance forever throughout your generations)" (Lev 10:9). "No priest shall drink wine, when he enters the inner court" (Ezek 44:21). And in the New Testament the Holy Spirit, through the Apostle Paul (1 Cor 6:10 and Gal 5:21), expressly said that drunkards will not inherit the kingdom of God.

The passion of drinking is a harmful passion for anyone, but for a clergyman it is many times more horrible. One needs to fight against this passion with all one's strength, estranging oneself from those who tempt, beckon, and pull one to drunkenness. Any wine that a priest uses should be a blessing, not a vice. Moderation and strict control over oneself are absolutely essential here; otherwise, this disease will grow and consume the soul and body of the one who is weak-willed. Yet, though drunkenness is such a grievous and deadly sin, there are very many in our time who scarcely pass a day without indulging their passion for drink. Therefore, Christ's Church, following the will of God, revealed in the canons both of the Apostles and of the Councils, forbids not only priests but all clergymen not merely to be drunken but even so much as to enter a tavern (that is, an establishment that exists only to provide alcohol to its customers) without need, or they may be subject to excommunication or even suspension.[29]

No Striker, Not a Brawler (Not Violent): These words have the same meaning as the expression in the Epistle to Titus Chapter 1, verse 7: "not self-willed, not quick-tempered." The minister of Christ must not only be no striker or brawler, but neither must he be rash or willful, and since these are the result of anger, he must avoid fits of anger. It is not appropriate, that is, that he be easily angered, without just reason, in any common or trivial matter. Much more monstrous is a priest who willfully enter into disputes or quarrels, whether about domestic matters or any other. All vain disputes and controversies about doctrine, which tend to display not truth but the ego, not God's glory but one's own, are forbidden to the clergy (1 Tim 6:4–5). "Remind them of these things, charging them before the Lord not to strive about words to no profit, to the ruin of the hearers" (2 Tim 2:14). "But avoid foolish and ignorant disputes, knowing that they generate strife. And a servant of the Lord must not quarrel but be gentle to all" (2 Tim 2:23–24).

A striker is not only a person who attacks his neighbor with his fists; he is also one who provokes others with words or gives offence to the weak, as it is written: "But when you thus sin against the brethren, and wound their weak conscience, you sin against Christ" (1 Cor 8:12). To the same purpose are the words of Christ concerning the careless and evil servant: "and begins to beat his fellow servants, and to eat and drink with the drunkards" (Matt 24:49).

Chrysostom, commenting on the word *striker* in his second moral on Titus, has these words: "The teacher is the physician of souls, but the physician strikes not, but tends and heals what is sick and wounded."[30]

PATIENT: To counter the above-mentioned faults of anger, strife, and quarrelling, the best and most effective remedy is patience, if it is true patience, springing from godly poverty of spirit and the fear of the Lord, made perfect not by extraordinary outward or bodily ascesis but by thoughts of inward humility. There is another kind of patience, which is feigned and hypocritical, put on to gain praise from men, but this is unpleasing to God and harmful to the soul. The Apostle Paul requires the priest to have true evangelical patience, whose fruits are the following: not to be quickly angered (even if there is justification for the anger); not to be confrontational and pugilistic but to give way; not to answer provocation with provocation but instead to act as St Peter spoke of Christ: "When He was reviled, did not revile in return" (1 Pet 2:23) and as Paul writes: "Being reviled, we bless; being persecuted, we endure; being defamed, we entreat" (1 Cor 4:12–13).

But if any evil report or slanderous accusation is brought against the priest—whether by any of his own parishioners or his brother clergymen—he should not keep silent, lest he seem to justify the slander and give cause for suspicion. Instead, he should prove his own innocence without anger or contention and then forgive his accusers. If he is forced to go to court, he can lawfully and with clear conscience strive to clear his own innocence without it being considered a breach of his duty to be patient. There is a good example of this in the words of the Apostle Paul in Acts chapter 24:10–21 and chapter 25:8, 10–11; and chapter 26:2–30.

NOT GREEDY FOR MONEY,[31] NOT ENVIOUS, NOT A LOVER OF MONEY: These vices are similar to one another, for since the love of money (according to the apostle) is *the root of all evil*, so greed, or the pursuit of unlawful gain, as well as envy are shoots springing from the same root, and it is through these shoots alone that the covetous spirit can be discerned. We may learn how grievous is the sin of covetousness, how terrible a passion in itself, and how destructive to the soul in its effects from the words of the apostle, who calls it the root of all evils and says in another place that covetousness is idolatry (Col 3:5).

If a priest of Christ is to be pure from such dreadful vices, he must have a single eye, free from evil, and the apostolic heart of Paul (Acts 20:33), not the eye or heart of Judas (John 12:6 and 13:2,27). Moreover, he must bear in mind this exhortation of the apostle: "But you, O man of God, flee these things and pursue righteousness, godliness, faith, love, patience, gentleness. Fight the good fight of faith, lay hold on eternal life, to which you were also called" (1 Tim 6:11–12).[32] Therefore, the Church, in order to turn away priests from improper gains, puts heavy canonical sanctions on such practices, threatening not only suspension but even excommunication and anathema against the offenders.

There are many ways of making money unlawfully that are unbecoming of the priestly order, but here we will mention only several:

1. Usury, when a priest of the Church gives out money with the expectation of it being returned with interest. This is forbidden by the canons under pain of suspension.[33]
2. Owning a tavern and profiting by it are prohibited by Canon IX of the Sixth Ecumenical Council.
3. Being involved in secular business is forbidden priests both by the word of God (2 Tim 2:4) and by the canons of the holy Fathers. In St Nicodemus's explanation of Apostolic Canon 81, in particular, we find the following: "A bishop or priest must not lower himself into political and secular affairs and business, but must confine his activities to diligently looking after the service and needs of the Church. So either let him be persuaded not do anything of the kind henceforth, or if he cannot be persuaded, let him be deposed."
4. Charging money for services and rites. The Lord Himself forbids this, saying, "Freely you have received, freely give"(Matt 10:8). Canon XXIII of the Sixth Council forbids taking money for the administering of the Holy Gifts. Apostolic Canon XXIX strictly forbids taking or giving money for ordination that is simony.

St Jerome, in his epistle to Nepotian, says the following: "If any clergyman becomes rich from being poor, becomes respectable from being lowly as a result of worldly business, flee him as the plague."

There is one more aspect of this that should be remembered as well—the danger possibly inherent in giving gifts of any kind. A gift is often given as a sign of one's respect, friendship, and love for someone who is close and dear. A gift should be chosen tastefully, tactfully. Something that is elegant, useful, memorable, and makes life beautiful is a wonderful present. Giving from one's heart to someone who is dear—this is a joy. However, giving a gift to one's superiors as a bribe is dishonorable, repulsive, and inexcusable. One must not accept gifts from subordinates or from strangers. Such a gift may become an advance payment, a deposit. In other words, the giver may expect preferential treatment in the future. It may place the priest under an obligation for a long time.

"One who rules his own house well, having his children in submission with all reverence" (1 Tim 3:4). The priest must never forget Eli, the high priest in the Old Testament, whom God punished for the sins of his profligate sons (1 Kings 3:11–14 LXX), and he should be very careful, lest he fall under a similar and still more severe punishment both for neglecting his own house and God's, that is, for the flock entrusted to him, which he is bound to guide along the way of salvation. The Apostle Paul requires that every prospective clergyman must first be tested and approved based on how well he rules his own house: "For if a man does not know how to rule his own house, how will he take care of the Church of God?" (1 Tim 3:5). Therefore, it is obvious that the priest has a duty to heed both his own house and the salvation of his flock, as it is written: "Know thoroughly the souls of your sheep, And you will set your heart on your flocks" (Prov 27:25 LXX).

Part of the priest's responsibilities regarding the running of his household is instructing his family in faith and holy living. His wife, according to the apostolic precept, must be "reverent, not slanderers, temperate, faithful in all things" (1 Tim 3:11). His children should also be "faithful ... not accused of dissipation or insubordination" (Titus 1:6). The canons insist on the same: "No one is to be ordained priest, who has not first brought all in his house to believe the faith."[34] A prospective priest can also not be married to a former prostitute, divorced woman, or widow, according to Apostolic Canon XVIII.

Chrysostom, in his second moral on Titus, writes the following: "If anyone cannot be a teacher even for his own children, how will he teach others? If he cannot rule those whom he has had with him, whom he has raised from infancy, and over whom he has authority both by law and nature, how can he profit others? Certainly, unless there was in the father the worst kind of softness or carelessness, he would not have allowed those under him to grow up evil."[35]

The proper ruling of the household must begin with the proper maintenance of the priest's house. A certain pastoral aura must be present in a priest's home, since it is a little church. Holy icons help to create this atmosphere. It is inconceivable that the dwelling of an Orthodox clergyman should be without icons. There may be only a few of them, but they must be present. These are the things that are indispensable for a priest's home: icons, the holy cross, the Gospel, spiritual books and images, an epitrachelion.

Sacred things in the home, such as icons, help a pastor to acquire a focused, prayerful state of mind. Preferably, the icons will be genuine icons, painted according to our Church's tradition, not modern replicas or cheap, crude imitations in tasteless, garish plating and ridiculous frames with hideous carvings. An Orthodox priest's icon corner should have no "Western" images, sculptures, bas-relief sculpture, or statuettes. If one's love of Western Catholic images is irresistible, then let them be placed not in the icon corner but rather on the walls, which is the place for pictures, not icons.

It has now become fashionable to collect ancient icons. Regrettably, only very few clergymen and churchly people collect, preserve, and value our church antiquities and, first and foremost, our chief treasure—the holy icon. However, it is not merely the collecting of icons that our clergyman must strive for but the creation of a churchly atmosphere in the home, the careful upkeep of sacred objects, and a grace-filled connection with spiritual images, which have seen centuries of prayer.

Oil lamps must burn before the holy icons and before them only! The ancient icon creates a grace-filled, prayerful atmosphere that is incomparable. If a pastor is not accustomed to such prayer, let him learn to pray before the ancient icons, and then he himself will be convinced that the icon inspires prayer specifically, rather than admiration for the external beauty of the image (as is often the case with Western art).

A house always testifies clearly to the culture and interests of its inhabitants. A clergyman's house, naturally, must have a distinctive character, as was already said above. It should be stressed that the pursuit of rich or stylish furniture and a striving toward luxury and extravagance are a flaw in a priest's life. Everything one has needs to be useful, of good quality, and in good taste, but without the taint of extravagance and low, coarse comfort. All forms of indulgence and the empty-headed accumulation of costly things must not have a place in the life of a clergyman.

A cultured person must first of all be orderly. Cleanliness surrounds him at all times and in all places. He does not leave things behind in disarray and does not bring anything in that might disrupt the decency of any place. A priest should keep his workplace and his dining table clean, and he should try to maintain cleanliness of public places, as well as his home.

Anything put in the wrong place or left wherever it happened to fall creates disorder, which will inevitably be reflected in the behavior of the house's inhabitants, especially children. Careless treatment of books or of any household object is unacceptable. One needs to always remember the labor of others and value and respect that labor. Order in the house and in the church indicates inner order and is conducive to concentrated work and vigilance.

Such orderliness will help the priest's household perform his pastoral duties. Times for prayer and for reading the word of God, and especially preparation for the Liturgy—these are very important aspects of pastoral service, and the household must be aware of their importance. The days and times when a priest leaves for a service or returns after a service must be peaceful and grace-filled; at these times it is especially necessary to avoid irritation, anger, and fuss over the trivialities of everyday life.

The exaltedness of the pastoral service, outside of church and at home as well, must be well known to all the members of the pastor's family, especially to the clergyman's wife. And he himself must provide an example of even-temperedness, peace, love, and order in the home. Mutual love, respect, friendship, and a sense of the loftiness of the pastoral duty must join all into a single Christian union, into a Christian family.

The taste, mentality, tact, and good manners of a clergyman's wife are very significant in this regard. In general, the appearance of a pastor's wife is far from unimportant. Many things in a priest's everyday life depend on the companion of his life, his friend who shares his cares and labors, who helps him and shares his pursuits and interests.

A priest's wife must love the church and its services, and her knowledge of Orthodox traditions must be broad. It is unpleasant to see the wife of a priest dressed in gaudy, extremely fashionable outfits and standing in church carelessly, with her head uncovered. A priest's wife is very important in his personal life. Neatness, cleanliness, peace, orderliness in everything complete equanimity and Christian love, friendliness to all who enter, sincerity, hospitality, strictness in questions of faith and life, a love for the beautiful, the sublime, and, of course, churchliness must be inherent traits of the inhabitants of a priest's house. A clergyman, together with his household and his wife in particular, must be a complete unit.

A clergyman's family should have its own good priestly traditions, which adorn life, making it churchly, Christian, spiritually rich, and beautiful. Of course, one ought to study the traditions of the clerical families in one's ancestry and be guided by them as much as possible, but every pastor's home can form its own traditions and habits as well.

The life of a clergyman and his family, as has already been mentioned, must be churchly in nature. In what is this churchliness expressed? In daily morning and evening prayers, in prayer before and after meals. In going to church on Saturdays, Sundays, and feast days; in observing fast days and Lenten periods; in lighting oil lamps before the icons. In celebrating feast days properly, free from worldly concerns and affairs. In preparing oneself and the house for great feasts. In a pious attitude toward holy objects such as *artos, antidoron*, and holy water. In reading literature edifying to the soul, in reading the word of God. In guarding one's tongue from ugly words and abusive language. In an interest in everything spiritual, salvific, and edifying. In a knowledge of the church year. In love for man, in acts of loving-kindness. In dedication, in peace, in joy. In mutual love and support. In adherence to all the Church traditions. In partaking of the Holy Mysteries. In abstinence. In respect for all who are in holy orders, in remembrance of the departed.

Not a Novice: A novice might be lifted up in pride and then fall into the same condemnation as the devil. Only the bishop can fully ensure that the priest is neither a novice nor insufficiently instructed in the doctrines of our holy faith. Therefore, nothing shall be here said of this, except what the Apostle Paul has admonished us concerning pride. For this also is one of the virtues required in a priest: he must not be proud, but humble-minded. The Apostle Paul requires this of the pastor of the Church, when he writes to Titus that a priest must not be self-willed (Titus 1:7), for self-will, or undue self-love, is precisely the source of pride and arrogance.

Lest the priest fall to the passion of pride, let him always remember that he is truly a minister of Christ and that Christ was humble and meek. He is a successor of the Apostles, who blessed those who reviled them (1 Cor 4:12). Furthermore, the priest must not deal with his parishioners in a lordly manner, for this was forbidden even to the Apostles by our High-Priest Himself, the Lord Jesus Christ.[36]

Humility is perhaps the greatest support for the pastor, manifested in all of his behavior and appearance. But this must be truly Christian humility, which is profound, not affected or ostentatious. Affectation, unctuous speech, sentimentality, pretended kindness— all of these are detestable forms of fraud. A priest cannot, as it were, step into a role—be one person inside the church and another when outside. Ambivalence here is unthinkable. There must not be any play-acting either within the church walls or without. The very life of a pastor is a sermon; it is the highest and best form of testimony; it is also a confession of faith. One must not deceive oneself or one's flock. One must live a churchly life both in the church and outside it, always clearly acknowledging one's responsibility for deviation from the norms of pastoral life and behavior, from the priestly vows, and from the oaths of the priesthood.

In our time—as perhaps in all times—there is a particular temptation that a young, inexperienced priest may easily fall prey to. "Crazy women," "myrrh-bearers," and "worshipers of batushka" chase after him, attend church only for him, see only him, are moved only by him, and so on. The end result is not service and prayer but a kind of sport. The priest himself must put a stop to these infatuations of his parishioners. A young pastor must not give cause for the rise of excessive praise toward himself, which quickly grows into worship, for his own sake and the sake of his parishioners. After all, for the Orthodox Christian the living image of Christ must always be first and foremost, but priests who are enamored of their own cult sinfully obscure this saving image.

Moreover He Must Have a Good Testimony among Those Who Are Outside Lest He Fall into Reproach and the Snare of the Devil: "Those who are outside" refers to those of other faiths and all those who do not believe in Christ, among whom the Early Church of the Apostles grew up as a lily in the midst of thorns. Who would be foolish enough not to realize the importance for the priest to truly shine, as St John Chrysostom teaches, brighter than the sun's rays? For if reproach from those outside the faith—which in our days is often enough reproach without reason—is something to be avoided, then how much more must any reproach from within the Church, especially from the priest's own flock, be a still greater snare and hindrance to his ministry? Chrysostom, in his forty-fourth moral on Acts 20, says the following: "This is the virtue of the teacher, to have his disciples witnesses of his good works."

Here it is also appropriate to note that the priest must not be "double-tongued," as the apostle requires of deacons in the same chapter (1 Tim 3:8) and thereby plainly implies of priests. "Double-tongued" refers not only to liars but also to slanderers and tattlers, even if there is justification for their tales. Here we must mention that dreadful kind of lying, joined with a desire for unlawful gain, which invents miracles, relates in God's name visions and apparitions that never occurred, and makes superstitious observations no better than sorcery. Let all such wicked impostors listen to this word of God: "Woe to those who prophesy from their hearts, but who see nothing at all!, Have you not seen a false vision and spoken worthless prophesies? Therefore say, 'Thus says the Lord: "Because your words are lies and your prophecies are worthless, therefore I am against you,"'" says the Lord. 'I shall stretch out My hand against the prophets who see lies and utter worthless things'" (Ezek 13:3, 7–9).

Other than the above-mentioned virtues, some others are by the Lord's commandment required of priests, as appropriate for their life and calling: "Be wise as serpents and harmless as doves" (Matt 10:16). "Do business till I come" (Luke 19:13). "By your patience possess your souls" (Luke 21:19). "Abide in Me, and I in you. As the branch cannot bear fruit of itself, unless it abides in the vine, neither can you, unless you abide in Me" (John 15:4). "I chose you and appointed you that you should go and bear fruit" (John 15:16). All these injunctions require the priests to follow the Lord Christ and make themselves one with Him by being prudent, modest, and discreet in their daily conversation with all people, by being attentive, correct, and indefatigable in the performance of the duties of their calling, and by being patient, strong-hearted, and unshakable in afflictions.

The Apostle Paul said, "To the Jews I became as a Jew, that I might win Jews ... to the weak I became as weak, that I might win the weak. I have become all things to all men, that I may by all means save some" (1 Cor 9:20, 22). "Therefore I run thus: not with uncertainty. Thus I fight: not as one who beats the air. But I discipline my body and bring it into subjection ..." (1 Cor 9:26–27). By this description of himself he not only sets himself before all priests as a model of wise and blameless conversation with people but also shows the special labors and exercises of an apostle. And yet, while he was engaged in such vast labors and in such arduous exercises, he was deeply humble-minded: "Brethren, I do not count myself to have apprehended; but one thing I do, forgetting those things which are behind and reaching forth unto those things which are ahead, I press toward the goal for the prize of the upward call of God in Christ Jesus" (Phil 3:13–14).

In the same way, it is the duty of every priest who exercises himself in all virtues not to think highly of himself; but, forgetting his own attainments, he must strive, like a good soldier of Jesus Christ, to still greater labors and still more arduous exercises that lie before him. The Apostle Paul urges us to do this when he says: "Brethren, join in following my example, and note those who so walk, as you have us for a pattern" (Phil 3:17).

Chrysostom, in his twelfth homily on Philippians, writes thus: "Nothing so spoils and ruins our success as the thought of the good we have done, for this begets in us a double evil: making us more remiss, and tempting us to pride. For this reason Paul, seeing how prone our nature is to sloth, teaches us humility by those words of his, 'Brethren, I do not count myself, and so on.'"

The Apostle Paul further exhorts the priest to be free from vices and adorned with all virtues needed for the priesthood, and his tone is almost commanding: "These things write I to you … so that you may know how you ought to conduct yourself in the house of God, which is the Church of the living God" (1 Tim 3:14–15). It is as if he had said: Timothy, know this! To be a priest in the house of the living God who will teach God's people, who will offer and minister Sacraments, who will intercede for the whole world, is to do a work that no man is fit for, other than the man whom I have described. For this he gives, in verse 16 of the same chapter, the following profound reason: "God was manifested in the flesh…." And in another place: "teaching us that, denying ungodliness and worldly lusts, we should live soberly, righteously, and godly in the present age" (Titus 2:12).

We will conclude this chapter with two general virtues, those of *faithfulness* and *wisdom*, which Christ Himself uses to describe His perfect steward, requiring the priest to have these virtues in abundance: "Who then is that faithful and wise steward, whom his master will make ruler over His household, to give them their portion of food in due season?" (Luke 12:42). Such faithfulness and wisdom consists in the following: the steward of God's house must not pass the time of his duty in eating and drinking, in getting drunk on the fruit of his stewardship, but he must diligently distribute food to others, he must teach the doctrines of the Church, he must minister the Sacraments, and he must pray to God. In all this he must not seek his own things "[but] the things which are of Christ Jesus" (Phil 2:21). Wisdom and faithfulness are such important aspects of the priest's duty that their presence is proof of all the other virtues and so these make the priest a servant "who does need to be ashamed" (2 Tim 2:15).

For the same reason the Apostle Paul, when he describes the calling of the apostle and his successor—a bishop or priest—requires him to have wisdom with faithfulness, writing thus: "Moreover, it is required in stewards that one be found faithful" (1 Cor 4:2). On the other hand, if this faithfulness and wisdom are lacking, what are the priest's virtues, but a mere semblance and mask? Or what is a steward but a whited sepulcher, showing off a beautiful and shiny veneer, but full of hypocrisy and lies on the inside? What can such stewards expect? Christ Himself answers: "The master of that servant will come on a day when he is not looking for him and at an hour that he is not aware of, and will cut him in two." What a terrifying punishment! "[He will] appoint him his portion with the hypocrites." This shall be the lot of the careless and unfaithful pastor. "There shall be weeping and gnashing of teeth" (Matt 24:50–51).

PART II

Ministering the Sacraments

CHAPTER 5

On the Sacraments in General

It is the priest's duty—before he administers any Sacrament—to teach the meaning of the Sacrament to the one who desires to receive it. He must teach him its purpose and the meaning of its outward form (its "matter"). For example, in baptism, he must teach him what is signified by the water, which of its own nature can only wash away bodily impurity; in chrismation, what is signified by the chrism, and so forth. For if the one participating in the Sacrament is left without instruction, he will not know himself what he receives; consequently, neither can he have faith, which naturally follows only after the knowledge of what is to be believed. Through faith we receive all those gifts of God that have been obtained for us by our Lord Jesus Christ (see Acts 10:43; 15:9 and Rom 3:22,25).[37]

The Apostle Paul indicates that it is impossible to have faith without being first taught what to believe with the following words: "How shall they believe in Him of Whom they have not heard?" (Rom 10:14). "Faith comes by hearing, and hearing by the word of God" (Rom 10:17). In other words, faith comes not from any human conversation but from the preaching of the word of God. Proof of this is given in the Acts of the Apostles, which describes the conversion of the Jews and Gentiles to the faith of Christ. The faith sprang up and was established by the hearing and reception of the preaching of the Gospel.

Since faith in the holy Sacraments is only one article of faith, dependent on others, the priest, as he explains the Sacrament, should question him who desires to receive it, whether he knows those articles of the faith that are necessary to salvation, such as the dogma of the Holy Trinity or the divinity of our Lord Jesus Christ, through the Creed. If not, then he must teach him these first, so he will be better able to understand the grace of the Sacrament he is about to receive and believe in it for his salvation.

In order to better understand this, it is proper to briefly describe the nature of faith that saves. Salvific faith is the undoubting reception of the Gospel of Christ in a heart brought to repentance. Such faith is called *unfeigned, heartfelt*, and *living*. Opposed to this is hypocritical faith, which is not felt with the heart, when a person does not really believe that the Gospel of Christ is true but still shows himself outwardly believing, as if he were a Christian. Such so-called faith is very offensive to God and may rightly be called unfaithfulness. The Apostle Paul describes such people thus: "They profess to know God, but in works they deny Him"—that is, by not believing Christ's Gospel, and by not believing Christ to be the Son of God—"being abominable, disobedient ... " (Titus 1:16).

Another kind of faith, no less harmful, is when a man believes that the Gospel of Christ is true but does not repent of his sins, refusing to seek pardon from God through Christ Jesus. Instead, he cares nothing for the holy life, existing without fear. Such faith—if indeed it can be called faith at all—is dead, lifeless, and unfruitful. Therefore, it is insufficient for salvation. The Apostle James writes of such faith in the second chapter of his general epistle. Thus, we may learn that to have saving faith means to believe without doubting in Jesus Christ, to know and believe in those articles of faith that are most necessary to salvation, and to live according to His holy commandment, performing good works, repenting wholeheartedly of all past sins, and asking God with the whole heart to forgive them, trusting in the blood of our Saviour Jesus Christ.

Therefore, it is plain that faith cannot exist without knowledge, nor can knowledge exist without preaching and instruction, and those who do not have faith in the Sacraments have neither virtues nor grace. Consequently, the ignorant should be taught the most necessary articles of faith before the priest administers the Sacraments to them.

For similar reasons, is it unlawful to perform the Sacraments for heretics who do not believe the doctrine of the Gospel—any Sacrament, in any way whatever—until they become converts to Orthodoxy, according to the Scriptures: "Do not give what is holy to the dogs, nor cast your pearls before swine" (Matt 7:6).

If priests—much more than laymen—must take care never to be guilty of serious sin, this is especially true when they minister any Sacrament, for otherwise the priest's sin—though it does not prevent the grace of God from flowing on him who worthily receives the Sacrament—becomes twice as heavy, because he, being impure, dares to touch the Holy Thing and the Ark of the Holy Spirit, Who dwells in the Sacraments. Even the priests of the Old Testament, who had to enter into the Tabernacle of Witness, were commanded by God to wash their hands and feet often, otherwise they would die (Exod 30:19–21 and 40:31). In this way, they were led by the ablution of bodily impurity to the washing away of the spiritual filthiness of sin. Therefore, the priests of the New Testament should always bear in mind this command of the apostle: "Let us cleanse ourselves from all filthiness of the flesh and spirit, perfecting holiness in the fear of God" (2 Cor 7:1).

It should go without saying that priests ministering the Sacraments must not be drunk. For if they have their mind darkened and so omit or change anything in the outward form pertaining to the essence of the Sacrament, as, for instance, in Baptism, if they forget to pronounce the words necessary for the completion of this Sacrament, they bring themselves under the severest condemnation of both God and His Church.

Let the priest therefore be exceedingly careful in no way to omit or change those things that pertain to the essence of any Sacrament and that are called its "matter" or "form." Let him also be careful to fulfill all the ritual actions of the holy Sacraments—and all the other rites and forms of the Church—with faith: "Without faith it is impossible to please [God]" (Heb 11:6). "Whatever is not from faith is sin" (Rom 14:23). Let him be totally attentive to the instruction and edification of him who is to receive the Sacrament; let him not hurry or fall asleep while performing the Sacrament, but let him always remember that terrifying denunciation: "Cursed is he who does the work of the Lord deceitfully" (Jer 48:10 (NKJV)).

Also, it is very important to correctly perform the blessing, sprinkling, anointing, wiping, and other physical actions in the Sacraments. All of these actions have a lofty spiritual meaning and they must be done with an awareness of their significance, without rushing, with devotion, reciting the words provided for the rite. Even walking around the holy altar table, or around the baptismal font, or an analogion during Sacraments should be done unhurriedly, reverently. Even such seemingly small details as the manner of raising one's hands at the liturgy are not unimportant. One should have a reverent and exalted appearance. Hands that are raised too high or are splayed out too far to the side create a poor impression. The hands lay emphasis on fervency of prayer, and their being raised on high must express the sincere prayerful disposition of the performer of the Sacraments.

Finally, the priest should remember that if selling holy things is utterly forbidden (he who asks even a penny from the communicant for the Eucharist must be suspended),[38] he should be rigidly careful to seek nothing in return for the ministration of Sacraments, according to the word of the Lord: "Freely you have received, freely give" (Matt 10:8). Instead, he must content himself with voluntary offerings—which should certainly be made!— according to the words of the Lord: "For a worker is worthy of his food" (Matt 10:10). Furthermore, the apostle says, "The Lord has commanded that those who preach the Gospel should live from the Gospel" (1 Cor 9:14).

If any priest, with the clergymen in his care, is so poor that he lacks enough money for bare necessities, he may ask his parishioners for assistance at some other time than when he is ministering Sacraments, in the spirit of the apostle's teaching: "Who ever goes to war at his own expense? Who plants a vineyard and does not eat of its fruit? Or who tends a flock and does not drink of the milk of the flock?" (1 Cor 9:7).

Note: The Sacrament of Ordination: The ministry of this Sacrament, that is, the laying on of hands for the priesthood, is the work of the bishop, and the clergyman ordained receives from him all instruction necessary for his order. As regards him, who comes to be ordained priest, what should be his character, and how he should prepare—these points have been handled throughout the chapters found in Part II, "Ministering the Sacraments."

CHAPTER 6

Some Important Aspects of Each Sacrament
in Particular, Beginning with the Sacrament
of Holy Baptism

When baptizing children, it is the priest's duty to see that the godfather or godmother is an Orthodox believer and knows those articles of the faith that are necessary to salvation, since the sponsor here stands in place of the baptized infant and answers for him before God (1 Pet 3:21), repeating the Creed. He or she is therefore responsible to teach the faith and God's law to the spiritual child, especially when the child has no other instructors. He or she must teach him the faith and God's law and do their best to remind him of his vows made at baptism, and of the virtue of that Sacrament, so that the child himself will learn and understand fully. All this of course cannot be done by any who are either ignorant of the faith themselves or members of another faith entirely.

Augustine, in his sermon CCXXII, writes the following: "Above all, I would have you, whether men or women, who have stood godfathers or godmothers to children, to know this. You are sureties for those whom you have taken up from the holy font; therefore, you must continually exhort them to keep purity, to love right, and to hold to love. Above all, be sure yourselves to know—and to teach your god-children—the Creed and the Lord's Prayer."

Young children, since they are as still uninstructed in the faith, are unfit for the office of godparent, while those of another faith are inappropriate, because the Creed with them is corrupted or mutilated, as with the Catholics and Protestants, and if they instruct the child, they will naturally pervert him to their own belief.

As for persons of more mature years who have decided to convert from Judaism, Islam, or Paganism, the priest must first teach them the articles of the Christian faith,[39] at the same time thoroughly refuting the soul-destroying error of their former faith, after which he must explain to them the grace and power of baptism. Then, with permission of his bishop, he may baptize them according to the order set forth in the Office-book. At the same time, if a person who desires to convert from false religion to the service of Christ happens to be ill, it is appropriate for the priest, even after a very slight instruction concerning the Holy Trinity and Jesus Christ, to baptize him, leaving to a future time, in case of recovery, the duty of instructing him more thoroughly.[40]

The practice of the Russian Church concerning rebaptism of other Christians has varied over the centuries. If there is any doubt, a priest must consult his bishop for the proper procedure.

The place of baptism ought to be in the church building, according to Canon LIX of the Sixth Ecumenical Council. However, in extreme cases, such as a child's illness or extreme weather in places where the church is far away, baptism may be performed in private houses.

When a child is dangerously weak or sick, if no priest is present, a layperson may baptize, that is, plunge the child into water, pronouncing the necessary words: "The servant of God (name) is baptized in the Name of the Father, and the Son, and the Holy Spirit." Therefore, the priest should teach his parishioners, and not men only but women also, whoever may be present at a birth, how to act in such circumstances. At the same time, he should instruct them always in such cases to give him immediate notice. Any person by whose negligence a child dies unbaptized is to be withheld from Communion for three years (Canon LXVIII of the Nomocanon) and must do penance of 200 prostrations daily, fasting Monday, Wednesday, and Friday of every week. However, every baptism performed by a layperson should, if the child lives, be completed by the priest with prayers and the other ceremonies appropriate to the Sacrament.

Stillborn children are not to be baptized, but the mother who miscarries should be examined by her confessor whether she has not been herself the cause of her own miscarriage by negligence or even, it may be, willfully. If it appears to be so, then the priest should impose penance on the woman, as for an involuntary homicide. If it has been willful, her penance is the same as for murder, according to the injunctions of the holy Canons.[41]

Foundlings should without question be baptized, unless there is some sufficient testimony of their prior baptism, even if a paper is found declaring them to be baptized, such paper having no name attached to it, nor naming the priest who performed the baptism.[42] Peter Mogila, Metropolitan of Kiev, in the Euchologion edited by him, gives this direction: "It is not amiss, when baptizing in such cases, to add some words in the form itself, thus: 'The servant of God (name) is baptized, if he be not already baptized, in the Name of the Father, and the Son, and the Holy Spirit.'"

We have said that godparents ought to do their best to teach children the faith and the law of God as soon as they begin to grow up. We also added, *if there is no other instructor*, for this duty belongs especially to the priest. Therefore, he will be only doing his duty, if every Sunday and feast day he calls the young people together to the church or school sometime in the afternoon and there instructs them.

This instruction should consist in the explanation of the Catechism, in which the first and chief thing is to remind them of their baptism, the vows given at baptism, whom they renounced, and to Whom they joined themselves. He should teach that they received remission of sins from their Heavenly Father because of the sacrifice of Jesus Christ, that they bound themselves to devote their lives in holy obedience to God, that they put on the new man, receiving new inclinations and powers by grace implanting in the understanding an enlightened knowledge of God, virtue, and true happiness of man, and in the heart love and zeal toward God and trust in the exceeding love of their Heavenly Father. He must teach them that the white robe given them at their baptism signified the innocence with which they were then endued, the lighted candle signifies the lighting of their heart with love for God, and so forth.

All this should be diligently instilled into them in their early years, so that no occasion arises for evil propensities to gather strength in them, but rather they will be continually stirred up to the love of virtue and godly living, for childhood, like a clay vessel, will give off the aroma of whatever substance fills it, whether pleasant or malodorous. Thus, while children are young, it is the duty of their godparents to teach them at home and of the priest still more to teach them in the church.

CHAPTER 7

The Sacrament of Chrismation

For chrismation, since it is administered together with baptism, nearly the same remarks are appropriate as for baptism itself:

1. The grace and intent of chrismation should be explained beforehand to the recipient, if he is old enough. In the case of children, when they are old enough to understand, they should be instructed in the importance of the Sacrament.

2. The priest must be provided with the proper chrism consecrated by a bishop, and he must be able to pronounce without hesitation the words at the anointing, and he must know what parts of the body are to be anointed.

3. The church is the place for the anointing with holy chrism, unless necessity requires otherwise.

4. Whenever there is a doubt that a person has been chrismated already, he is to be anointed without hesitation.

5. No layperson can administer this Sacrament, even if there is the danger of death.

6. As for heretics or schismatics who return to the true faith, in order to know which of them should be chrismated and which should be received with confession alone, the priest should always consult his bishop.

CHAPTER 8

The Sacrament of Confession

The Sacrament of confession exceeds all the other Sacraments that the priest has to perform in difficulty and responsibility, for it requires a specific skill set and very great discretion and diligence. In this office, the priest is a spiritual physician whose work is with those who are sick of many different diseases. Often in one and the same soul there are many old and putrefying wounds that have corrupted the entire substance of the soul and all its vital powers. Furthermore, the tragedy of the people afflicted with such diseases is that they either feel no weight from them or they conceal them from their physician or, after putting themselves into his hands, they do not tolerate the necessary medicine. Therefore, it will also be proper to give instruction on this Sacrament more at length, especially underlining the priest's duties before confession, during confession (when this Sacrament is completed by absolution), and after confession.

BEFORE CONFESSION

Since confession is especially encouraged during the four fasting periods, the priest should use every opportunity during these fasts to teach his parishioners the essence of true repentance. In other words, he must show them what the penitent must do.

1. The penitent must acknowledge his sins, and recall to mind, as much as he can, all that he has done wrong by deed, word, and thought, whether committed knowingly and willfully, for which his conscience pricks him, or in ignorance.

2. Having acknowledged his sins, he must repent and be sorry for having so angered the Lord and subject himself to His righteous judgment.

3. He must confess them before God in prayer every day, and before the priest as well, since the priest alone has the power of absolution.

4. When he asks mercy of God, he must remember Jesus Christ crucified and trust only to His mercy for the remission of sin.

5. He must firmly resolve not to relapse into sin, but to begin a new life, according to God's commandments, and he must strive to bring forth worthy fruits of repentance.

He who has fallen into any grievous sin, especially into any fierce or vehement passion of the flesh, should not wait for the fasting periods to confess, but he should run as soon as possible after his fall with true repentance to God and go to confession. Having thus received for his wound whatever treatment is suitable, he must pray to God with his whole heart to forgive him. For in this way the violent impulses of passions will be bridled, and sin prevented from gaining ground in our hearts, even if it is already well established and easily masters us. Through confession the passion's hold over the penitent is loosened. Therefore he may, by God's grace, obtain deliverance from his cruel tormentor, but without confession he would have no hope of such deliverance. For this reason, Jesus the son of Sirach writes thus: "Do not delay to turn to the Lord, and do not put it off from day to day; for suddenly the wrath of the Lord will come forth, and in the day of vengeance, you will perish" (Sir 5:7).

St John Chrysostom, in his twenty-second moral on Hebrews, writes the following: "To put off confession is ruin and fear, but not to put it off is certain and sure salvation" (and more of the same, see the rest of the homily).

"By the law is the knowledge of sin" (Rom 3:20; 7:7). Therefore, whoever seeks to know his own faults should look into the mirror of the Ten Commandments (James 1:25), and it is very necessary that the priest should explain the commandments to those parishioners who are preparing for confession, encouraging them to examine themselves in light of each commandment. Have they done that which this commandment requires or have they neglected it and left it undone? Have they done that which this commandment forbids? The injunctions and prohibitions of the commandments in their widest sense will only be understood as well as the priest explains them. And not only must the sins themselves be known but also their results, such as the wrath of God, the punishments prepared for the sinner, and the fearful curse both in this world and in the world to come (Deut 27:26), from which the Son of God delivered us by drinking His most bitter cup of suffering (Gal 3:13).

If repentance is sincere, it cannot exist without loathing and aversion for sin, and true penitents will not only hate the sinful acts themselves but will also hate and avoid the places, instruments, persons, and all other circumstances that lead to sin. Moreover, if the penitent sinner has a vivid sense of God's anger against him, he cannot help but feel confusion and terror, even to the wasting of his body and the impairing of its strength (see Psalm 36:3–4, 11). In the true penitent, conversely, repentance always produces heartfelt sadness and tears, for tears are like blood pouring from a wounded soul, and where they are lacking, it is a clear sign that the soul thinks there is either no wound at all or only a small one. The same genuine repentance will further inspire asceticism, fasting, and simple living (Ps 100:5,10 LXX), for the man that struggles turns away from all that is sweet and pleasant, and such a fast is in the spirit of the Church, well pleasing to God.

Genuine confession should represent the exact state of the soul as in a mirror; therefore, whoever confesses before a priest should not conceal any of the sins that trouble his conscience neither should he try to add nor diminish their seriousness. At the same time, he should not excuse himself or try to find extenuating circumstances to lessen his fault, such as weakness, necessity, or ignorance. Of course, he must never blame his own sin on another person (Gen 3:12–13). Even if he has partners in his sin, the priest should never seek to find out who they are nor should the penitent reveal their names; otherwise, it will not be the confession of a sinner, but the self-justification of a Pharisee and an accusation of sin that the other people may have already confessed (in which case they are justified as was the publican (Luke 18:11,14)). Such a good confession is not only the natural fruit of sincere and heartfelt contrition and faith in Christ, but it is also clearly grounded in the word of God (Num 5:7; Prov 28:13; John 1:9) and illustrated by countless examples from the Scriptures (see Neh 9:2; Matt 3:6; Acts 19:18).

However, confession without faith in Christ—faith in the strictest and most proper sense means trust in Christ's mercy—is no less dead than a body without a soul. The example of Judas proves this clearly and convincingly enough. He betrayed Christ, and yet he repented and confessed his sin not merely in the ear of one other person but publicly before all, even returning the pieces of silver. However, since he did not seek God's mercy as did Peter, with hope in the Son of God who allowed Himself to be betrayed for that very purpose, his confession did him no good, and it was followed not by absolution but by despair and the noose. Truly, how can such faith not be necessary to repentance when it brings peace to the troubled sinner and frees him entirely from condemnation to torment? (Rom 5:1 and 8:1).

Concerning such faith, St Justin the Martyr, in his fortieth *Question*, says, "Through repentance and faith in Christ a man receives remission of the sins that he has committed." Clement of Alexandria, in the second book of his *Stromata*, has these words: "To true repentance it is indispensable that we cease from our sins and believe." St Ambrose, in his first book on repentance, writes thus: "Repentance cannot be genuine, unless you believe that your sins will be forgiven." In the tenth book of the same work, as well as his commentary on Luke chapter 24, he writes the following: "It is not tears only that God requires, but also faith. Tears truly are profitable, but only if we come to know Christ."

Finally, the priest must teach his penitent the necessity of forming a firm resolution not to return again to sin, as the dog does to his vomit (2 Pet 2:22). Instead, he must lead a new and virtuous life, according to God's commandments. With regard to sins that have become confirmed by habit, the man who is held by them must train himself to become proficient in the virtue contrary to his habitual sin. By doing this, he will at least weaken and reduce his sinful habit, if not eradicate it, since it cannot be removed completely in such a short time. Furthermore, it is necessary for him to show that he truly is fighting against the sin ruling over him and that he fights the war against his lusts in earnest. For this reason, the man who is enslaved by a sinful habit—unless he fights against it—cannot be considered truly penitent and is not ready for absolution, not having yet begun to free himself from the bonds of sin (Rom 6:16).

St Athanasius, in his commentary on the parables of the Gospels, writes the following: "Repentance is not the bending of the knees, but self-restraint from sin, with self-abasement and mortification and tears of sorrow and prayer to God to forgive us what we have done amiss. This is signified by the very word μετάνοια (*that is*, "*turning*"), that it turns the mind from evil to good." And St Ambrose says, "This is penitence: to weep for past sins, and to avoid doing things worthy of weeping in the future."

In addition to such explanations of the nature of confession, the priest should admonish his parishioners that every one who has any quarrel with another must be reconciled. In other words, if he has done anything wrong to any one, he must repair it, as much as possible (Matt 5:23–24). St John Chrysostom writes the following: "If in thought you have injured anyone, then in thought be reconciled. If by word you have injured anyone, then by word be reconciled, but if by deed, then be reconciled also by deed."

Otherwise, if a person can make amends, but does not, he is not truly penitent; consequently, even if the priest were to absolve him, he would remain unabsolved with God. This is especially applicable to the sin of stealing, of which it is said, "There is no absolution for the sin, unless the thing stolen be restored." But if a man has himself been wronged by anyone else, then it is his duty to forgive, so that he will obtain forgiveness of his sins from God, since his debt before God is immeasurably greater, not of *denarii* but of heavy *talents*, and so not suffer the fate of the cruel debtor in the Gospel (Matt 18:35).

If the priest sees that any of his parishioners are careless about repentance, he should warn them about God's displeasure increasing day by day, even impending over their heads (Rom 2:4–5; Isa 45:11). With such warnings he should let them know that deferred repentance rarely finds opportunity, sometimes because such people are through God's just judgment cut off suddenly and sometimes because when they come to die, even if the death itself is not sudden, there are many things, such as the severity of sickness, the terror of death, and the lamentations of their surrounding friends, which scarcely leave it possible for them reflect on their life or to develop the kind of disposition that is necessary for producing true repentance, which includes faith and trust in Christ. Besides, it may well happen that the very thought of the negligence of their past lives will incline them to despair, not to hope. Finally, he should teach them that repentance under the pressure of pain and fear, even though apparently genuine, is not enough, because in such cases, it is not that we leave our sins but that our sins leave us. Therefore, repentance must not be put off, but as soon as someone feels himself to have sinned, he should immediately repent.

AT THE TIME OF CONFESSION

The priest should be cautious not to confess strangers from other parishes who seek to avoid their own pastor from shame, especially if they have not battled a habitual sin but remain unrepentant in spite of many warnings. Therefore, unless there is some lawful reason for receiving them to confession, he should admonish them and send them back to their own spiritual father.

Nothing can be more careless and shameless than the practice of some priests who receive to public confession as a group not only little children under ten years of age but together with them many others, including young people of both sexes who are already in their teens or older. Without questioning them about sins that they have committed and without informing them about sins they may have committed in ignorance, such priests indiscriminately read the prayer of absolution over them all together. If the reason for such disorderly practice is the pretense that the number of people to confess is too great for the priest to get through in one day before communion, as is our custom, the answer is that there is nothing to prevent him from confessing those who are preparing to communicate two or three days or even a whole week beforehand. In that case, however, he should admonish his penitents that if their conscience still accuse them of anything, or if they fall into any fresh sin before communion, they should come and confess a second time, but this we trust will occur rarely.

When the priest questions the penitent regarding his sins, he should be cautious how he lists the different kinds and distinctions of sins, especially sins of the flesh, or he may unwittingly acquaint the penitent with a sin of which he was previously ignorant. The safe way is to question only in general terms, putting the penitent in mind of the Ten Commandments and what is contrary to them. The same can be said regarding the details and circumstances of any sin that is confessed. In order not to make the sin any worse in the future, the priest should be very careful to ask no unnecessary questions. Instead, he should diligently try to find the causes leading to that particular sin, so that he could suggest a remedy suitable to the wound. In other words, by doing this he will teach the penitent to nip the sin, so to speak, in the bud to give it no opportunity for further growth, but instead, if he desires to be safe from that deadly plant, to pluck it up by the roots. This will also help the priest find the most appropriate penance for his penitent, suitable to the nature and cause of the sin.

When hearing confessions, if the priest perceives that the sinner is still hardened and cold in his heart, he must try to alarm him with the examples of the axe of God's wrath laid at the root of the barren tree (Matt 3:10), the cursing and cutting down of the fig tree (Mark 11:14, 21; Luke 13:7), the judgment to come, which shall be terrible even to the righteous (1 Pet 4:17–18), the loss of the joys of heaven, the fierceness and the eternity of the torments of hell, the gnashing of teeth, the outer darkness, the worm that never dies, the sighing and weeping without end, the everlasting and unquenchable fire (Matt 25). Furthermore, let him terrify the sinner by the examples of the condemned angels, who did not remain in their sinless state, the flood that drowned the whole world, the fire that burned Sodom and Gomorrah (2 Pet 2:4–6), the plagues and deaths that visited the disobedient and murmuring Israelites in the wilderness because of their unbelief. He must say with the apostle, "Now these things became our examples, to the intent that we should not lust after evil things as they also lusted" (1 Cor 10:6). Lastly, he should offer the tremendous example of Jesus Christ Himself, the pledge of our salvation, Who was delivered up and died upon the Cross, for sins not his own but ours. By doing this, the priest will show the penitent, as in a clear glass, what the just and intolerable wrath of God will inflict on the impenitent sinner.

But if the priest notices that the penitent doubts or even despairs of God's mercy, he must comfort him and strengthen him with the thought of God's infinite mercy (Sir 1:23; 2:11), with the promises given us, even with an oath, that God wills not the death of the sinner (Ezek 33:11), but instead to save sinners, He sent His Son into the world (John 3:16; Matt 9:13). The priest should remind him that Christ's Blood, shed for all (1 John 1:7; 2:2), washed us clean of sins and redeems us, according to the riches of the grace of God (Eph 1:7; Col 1:14). Furthermore, the priest should comfort him with the example of sinners who found mercy in ancient times, including David after his adultery and murder, Manasseh after his idolatry and other grievous sins, Peter after his apostasy, Paul after his persecution of the true faith, the publican, the woman taken in adultery, the thief on the cross, and others without number.

Tertullian, in his discourse on repentance, has these words: "Not only does God command us to repent, but He also exhorts us to it. He encourages us with the promise of a reward unto salvation. He even confirms it with an oath, so that we will believe Him without doubt. O, how blessed are we, for whose sake God even gives an oath! O, how thrice-wretched are we if, even when God has sworn to us, we still do not believe Him!"

St Cyprian of Carthage, in his discourse on communion, writes thus: "Neither the weight of transgressions, nor the shortness of time, not even if it is the last hour of life (assuming true contrition of heart and genuine change from evil desires to good), exclude us from forgiveness. In His infinite abyss of mercy, Love receives all returning prodigals as a mother, and God's grace, at whatever time they turn from sin, receives all penitents."

As the priests of the Old Testament were commanded carefully to distinguish between one kind of leprosy and another (Lev 13), so should the priests of the Gospel carefully distinguish between different sins. They must determine how dangerous is this particular spiritual leprosy, whether or not it has gone deep into the inward substance of the soul, whether it has infected many of the soul's powers and senses, whether it has perverted the image of Christ that must be in every true Christian (Gal 4:19), whether it has deprived the soul of the sap of life, that is, of the grace of the Holy Spirit, the life of the soul. For some sins are greater, others less. Some are deadly, some are not (a deadly sin is compared by St John Chrysostom to a putrefying corpse). Some are committed ignorantly and involuntarily, while others are done willingly, knowingly, with a concrete purpose, even with, as it were, a high hand against God (Num 15:30). If such sins are not eradicated by true repentance, but are left from day to day to go on increasing, they will finally become that fearful sin against the Holy Spirit that is unforgiveable both in this world and in the world to come (Matt 12:31–32; Heb 6:4, 10:26,29; 1 John 5:16). Moreover, some sins actually tyrannize the sinner (Rom 6:12, 16), among which the first place belongs to sins of habit.

This examination of sins is indispensable for a priest, so that he will know what to do with the sinner and how to best treat him. The priest of the Old Testament, by God's commandment, after inspection of the leprosy, pronounced those whose sores were not dangerous and had not infected all the body to be clean, allowing them to return to the people of God, while those whose disease seemed dangerous they shut up in a separate place and inspected again at intervals of seven days. Those who were obviously infected with real leprosy were declared to be unclean and expelled from the assembly of the chosen people. The priests of the New Testament do the same: those sinners whose sins either are of the lesser kind—that is, involuntary and committed in ignorance or, though grievous and deadly, those beginning to be healed by true repentance—they absolve and declare ready to commune of the Holy Mysteries. However, in cases when the sins are greater and further rooted in the soul by habit or in cases when repentance is doubtful, it is proper to defer absolution in order to sober up the penitent with the purpose of leading him to repentance. Or, if absolution is given in these cases, the penitent should still by all means be forbidden to commune and examined frequently at intervals to ascertain whether by the help of God's grace they have been resisting their evil habit and have freed themselves from its yoke. Finally, in some cases there is grievous sin and no doubt that repentance is only feigned. Such people, being incurably diseased, must not be absolved, but the priest must try to frighten them with God's fearful judgments (of which we have spoken already above). The priest must make it abundantly clear to them that if they do not truly repent and submit to penance, they will be excommunicated from Christian communion, even as the lepers of old were cast out from the nation of Israel.

St John Chrysostom, in his eighty-third sermon on Matthew, writes as follows:

> Let no one inhuman, no one rough and unmerciful, least of all any one unclean approach here. This I say not only to you who seek to receive Communion, but also to you whose ministry it is to give it. For there is need to say the same thing to you also, in order that you may use great care and diligent examination before distributing these Gifts. No slight torment is that which awaits you if you knowingly admit any one who is still confirmed in his sins to approach to the Communion of this Table, for His Blood will be required at your hands. Though any ruler, though a king himself seeks to approach unworthily, forbid him, do not admit him. Your power here is greater than his. If you have been set to guard some clean spring of water for the

flock, and you saw that swine covered with stinking mud were running into that clean water, doubtless you would not allow them with their mud to defile it. Here is not a spring of water, but of Blood, the Holy Spirit Himself, that is given to your keeping. If you see anyone defiled with sin, more putrid than mud, approach without penitence, will you not stop him? Will you not forbid him? And what pardon can you ever have for such negligence? It is for this that God has been pleased to honor you with the great dignity of the priesthood, that you should with the utmost diligence guard these Mysteries. This is your merit, this is your fortitude, this is your crown! Not to move about in the church in beautiful and consecrated vestments. But will you say, How can I know what is in this or that man? I do speak of those whom you do not know, but of those whom you do. Listen to something fearful and horrible that I will say: It is better to be possessed by a devil, that to be like them, of whom St. Paul says, that they "tread under foot the Son of God, and change the Blood of the covenant into an unclean thing, and do despite to the Spirit of grace." Therefore, he is far worse than one possessed, who, knowing himself to be defiled, and without penitence, approaches. Those who are possessed are blameless in that they are tormented of the devil and will never be punished with torment for that, but they who approach communion unworthily will be given over to everlasting torments. Therefore, we repel at once all those whom we know to be approaching unworthily. Let no one be admitted to communicate, unless he is of the disciples. Let no one with a heart defiled like Judas receive the bread, lest he suffer a similar fate to him. This is the Body of Christ, and this multitude of the congregation too is His Body. Be diligent, then, O Priest, when you serve in the Mysteries, lest you anger the Lord by being careless to purify this Body, lest you give them a sharpened sword instead of bread. But if any one approaches this table out of obstinacy or madness, repel him. Fear not: fear God, not man. If you fear man, you will be despised even by that very man whom you fear, but if you fear

God, then you will be honored by men also. But if you dare not to repel him yourself, inform me. I will not allow any such presumption. I would sooner lay down my life, than give any one the Lord's Body unworthily. I would rather have my own blood poured out, than allow any to communicate of That most pure Blood unworthily. If anyone who is defiled approaches, and you do not know it, then this is no fault of yours, if you have done everything you can to prevent it. I have been speaking of notorious and open sinners, whom if we correct, God will sooner or later reveal to us also, if we not know them. However, if we admit open sinners without penitence, what reason will there be for God to reveal to us the others? All this I say, not to the end that we should only refuse to admit or expel sinners, but that we should amend them and bring them back to the right way, to be watchful and diligent for the good of all, for thus we shall both gain God's mercy upon ourselves and find a greater number of those who may worthily communicate. And so for our own diligent care of others, we shall receive a great reward.

Methodius, Patriarch of Constantinople, writes the following in the Nomocanon: "There are many who confess and grieve, but still either by the force of nature, or of evil disposition, or evil habit, again relapse into their previous sin. These should always go and confess, as often as they fall, but they should never be admitted to Communion, even though they perform the penances that they have received from the Priest who bound them."

There are also those who repent hypocritically. These include the following:

1. Those who continue in enmity and will not be reconciled with their neighbors.
2. Thieves who will not restore what they have stolen.
3. Malefactors who confess their crimes to the priest, but pretend innocence in court.
4. All who conceal from their confessor any part of their transgressions.

5. All who after sufficient admonition and with knowledge of the truth still persist in not giving up any sinful habit, such as fornication, drunkenness, covetousness, or any other vice.

At the time of absolution, a priest may administer penances, consisting in some particular good works such as prayer, fasting, and almsgiving. It is not that the penances make satisfaction to God for sin, for Christ by offering Himself in sacrifice to God the Father "has perfected forever those who are being sanctified" (Heb 10:14), but through penances, we have the opportunity to show "fruits worthy of repentance" (Matt 3: 8) and lay the foundations of a virtuous life. Most importantly, we are enabled to take all possible means to kill the remaining roots of the sin that we have confessed, that is, those enticements that generate the sin and above all the habit, if the sin has become habitual. Therefore, penances should be chosen carefully, so that the virtues prescribed will be those most effective against the sin for which the penance is imposed. For example, the covetous should be required to give alms, the sensual should fast, the weak in faith and hope should be given prayer rules, and so on.

However, in doing this it will be necessary also to have some consideration for the circumstances of the penitent. For instance, a poor man will find it difficult to give alms or a shopkeeper or any other whose business requires constant attention will have difficulty performing long prayers. And on this point we have an example given to us by the great preacher of repentance, St John the Baptist (Luke 3:11, 14).

St John Chrysostom, in his tenth moral on Matthew chapter 3, writes the following: "How can we bring forth fruits worthy of repentance, but by doing what is contrary to our sins? Have you stolen what is another's? Begin then to give away what is yours. Have you lived a long time in fornication? Abstain even from a lawful bed. Have you injured anyone by deed or word? Then bless them that curse you, and strive to soften them that strike you, both by serving them, and by doing them good." Augustine, in *De Dogma Ecclesia*, has these words: "Satisfaction in penitence consists in this: that we eradicate the causes of sins, and leave no entrance for their impulses."

For those whose sins have been secret, the penance imposed should be secret also; otherwise, if the penance is public, it will make the sin public (on this point, see Canon xxxiv of St Basil the Great). But open sinners, such as harlots, adulterers, sorcerers, or drunkards, whose sinfulness is notorious to all, must have a public penance. Otherwise, if they are admitted to the communion of the Body and Blood of Christ with other Christians, it would cause a new scandal, in addition to the one already caused by the notoriety of their sins. In effect, there would be no distinction between the public sinner and someone who has always lived a good Christian life.

Furthermore, the degree of the penance should depend on the seriousness of the sin, its cause and circumstances, the age of the penitent, and most of all on the manner of repentance manifested by him, whether warm and heartfelt or cold. For where the heart is warm, even a long penance required by the canons may be shortened; while, on the contrary, if the heart is cold, even a short one should be lengthened (see Canon XII of the First Ecumenical Council and Canon CII of the Sixth).

Chrysostom, in his fourteenth moral on 2 Corinthians, writes thus:

> I do not require length of time, but amendment of soul. Show me only this, that you are softened, that you are changed, and that is everything. But if this is not so, there is no profit in time. For neither do we inquire how long a wound has been bound up, but whether it is at all the better for it. If it has done its work, in however short a time, the bandage is not to be kept on longer; but if not, then, even if it has been on even ten years, it must be kept on still. And so let this be the term for absolution when he who has been bound is corrected.

And since penance is not strictly a satisfaction to God, a penitent may be absolved even without any penance, if he sincerely and with tears promises never to return to his sin. So John the Baptist imposed no penance on the publicans who repented other than telling them to act fairly according to the laws prescribed for their office (Luke 3:13). Chrysostom, in his sermon on the Blessed Philogonus, Bishop of

Antioch, has these words: "I testify and pledge myself to you, that if any one of us who were under sin departs truly from his former evil ways and wholeheartedly promises God never again to return to them, God requires nothing more for further satisfaction, for He is merciful."

AFTER CONFESSION

The following rules are to be observed:

1. The priest is never to disclose to anyone a sin confessed to him, nor even allude to it in general terms, or in any other way, but he must keep it to himself as a thing simply sealed up and consigned to silence forever; otherwise, he subjects himself to a heavy judgment.

2. The priest should never speak judgmentally to the one who confesses, but he must remember that he is not the judge of the penitent, but only the witness of his repentance, a servant appointed to minister to the salvation of men (2 Cor 4:5). The man who sins, sins against God alone (Ps 99:5 LXX), and he who repents, receives pardon from God alone (Mark 2:7). The priest is merely the intermediate instrument through whom God works.

3. With regard to priestly authority, let him understand that it is spiritual, not temporal (John 18:36), consisting not in lordship but in service (Matt 20:25–27). Therefore, he ought to exercise it with humility and tears (Acts 20:19), with gentleness (2 Tim 2:24–25), to edification, not to destruction (2 Cor 13:10).

4. Therefore, the priest should not have a condescending manner, but instead should pray to the Lord for those who confess to him, and he must struggle in heart day and night until Christ is formed in them (Gal 4:9) and dwells through faith in their hearts (Eph 3:17). To this end, he must use all his powers and means to teach them true repentance to God both in word, deed, and faith in our Lord Jesus Christ. He must inspire them not to return to their former sins but to be from this moment vessels sanctified for honor, appropriate for the Master's use, prepared for every good work (2 Tim 2:21).

St John Chrysostom, in his sermon concerning the fall of the first man, has the following: "Sin not, O man, after you have received pardon. Wound not yourself after you have been healed. Defile not yourself after grace, but remember that after pardon once received, sin is more grievous. A wound that has been once healed, but breaks out afresh, gives the sharpest pain. He offends God much more, who, after he has been cleansed by grace, again defiles himself. Therefore, he who sins after pardon deserves no mercy. He who wounds himself after being cured is unworthy of help. He who defiles himself after receiving grace is unworthy of purification."

From these reflections, everyone must clearly see how terribly those priests act when they deprive parishioners of communion—or even do not allow them to kiss the cross or receive antidoron or take part in any other rite—merely because of petty anger or personal insult. Such priests sin grievously because by all such acts the name of God is dishonored, and holy things, which are delivered to us as pledges or signs of His grace, are turned into instruments of malice or vile covetousness.

Gregory the Preacher, in his twenty-fourth epistle, has these words: "If any one unrighteously or uncanonically separates another (from the holy Mysteries), he condemns himself." Augustine, in his sixteenth sermon on the lord's discourses, has the following: "You have begun to consider your brother no better than a publican, and you bind him on earth, but see if you do righteously in binding him, for justice shall tear the bands of injustice asunder."

As for sick people, whether in his own parish or strangers if their own priest is not at hand, any priest who happens to be within reach may freely hear their confessions and give them absolution for all manner of sins. Even if they are under formal excommunication, if they are in imminent danger of death and truly penitent, the priest may give them Holy Communion, with this proviso, that any person so absolved, if he does not die, must perform the penance appointed to him after his recovery and after having performed it, he must present himself again to his former confessor, according to the canons.[43]

CHAPTER 9

The Sacrament of Holy Communion and Some General Remarks Regarding the Serving of the Divine Liturgy

Before giving the Communion of the most holy Body and Blood of Christ, the priest should instruct those who wish to commune that the Body and Blood of Christ is not merely called this symbolically, but truly and indeed is His Body and His Blood, in the forms of bread and wine, for the grace of the Holy Spirit accomplishes this Sacrament, and to Him nothing is impossible. Our Saviour Christ Himself instituted this Communion before His passion at His last supper, expressly for this purpose: that faithful Christians partaking of this Sacrament might partake of Christ Himself and so be worthy sons by adoption of the Father in heaven and true members of Christ's Body the Church, and so they might commemorate the saving sufferings and death of Christ and give Him sincere thanks as their Redeemer (Luke 22:19; 1 Cor 11:24–26). For this reason, Communion is called also the Eucharist, that is, the Service of Thanksgiving.

The priest should also teach them that whoever receives this Communion worthily "has eternal life" (John 6:54) for Christ Himself is communicated to such and lives in them (verse 56) and promises even after their deaths to raise them up again, as precious vessels, as dwellings pleasant to Himself, at the last day. On the contrary, they who receive unworthily receive it to themselves unto condemnation and sin like the Jews who betrayed the Body of Christ and shed His

Blood. They subject themselves to God's judgment, to punishments both temporal and eternal (1 Cor 11:27–30; John 13:27).[44] With such people it often happens that the last state is worse than the first (Matt 12:45).

Therefore, when the priest intends to celebrate this awesome and tremendous Sacrament, he must prepare himself with all purity and administer it with reverence and godly fear. He must also, without fail, teach those preparing for Communion to approach it with purity and reverence, every person diligently examining his own conscience (1 Cor 11:28), that is, whether he has truly repented, whether he wholeheartedly hates the sins he committed, for Christ cannot abide in a heart defiled by sin (2 Cor 6:14–15), whether he has begun to live to Christ, whether he perceives in himself the fruits of justification obtained by Christ's Blood, that is, peace with God and joy in his heart in the Holy Spirit (Rom 14:17; 15:13), for all these effects are produced in a person by living and saving faith. Every person must test himself by these criteria if he wishes to commune worthily, as the apostle teaches in 2 Corinthians chapter 13, verse 5.

Basil the Great, writing to a certain priest concerning the Divine Services, writes the following:

> Study, O Priest, to show yourself a workman unashamed, rightly dividing the word of truth. Take care never to stand in the congregation having enmity against anyone, lest you drive away the Comforter. On the day that you are to serve do not talk much, do not hurry, but remain in the church, praying and reading holy books, until the hour when you must perform Divine Liturgy. Then, stand with a contrite and pure heart before the holy altar. Do not look around here and there, but with fear and trembling stand before the King of Heaven. Do not try to shorten the prayers for the sake of pleasing men. Pay no attention to those around you, but look solely to the King Who is lying before you and to the heavenly powers standing round about Him … Pay attention to the One before Whom you stand, be attentive to how you serve.

St John Chrysostom, in his sermon on the Blessed Philogonus, Bishop of Antioch, writes thus:

> If we approach with faith, we will doubtless behold Christ lying as it were in the manger, for here also is laid the Body of the Lord, not wrapped in swaddling clothes as then, but clothed on all sides with the Holy Spirit. Those who are enlightened by faith will understand what I say. There the Magi, who came, only worshipped, but you, if you come with a pure conscience, are permitted also to receive Him and to depart home. Approach, therefore, and bring Him gifts, not the gifts of the Magi, but much more precious gifts. They brought gold; you bring chastity and other virtues. They brought frankincense; you bring the spiritual frankincense of pure prayer. They brought myrrh; you bring self-abasement, humility, and alms. And if you approach with these gifts, then you will partake with a confident hope, and you will enjoy the sweetness of this holy table. Let us not do this then to the wounding or condemnation of our soul, but for our salvation. I now testify and entreat you. Cleanse yourselves first in any manner you can, and only then approach the Holy Mysteries.

In his eighty-third sermon on Matthew, he further says the following:

> Let no one half dead approach, nor anyone unsound, but all with a glowing heart and flaming spirit, lit and burning. For if the Jews ate the Passover standing, with their feet shod and their staves in their hands, in haste, then how much more must you now be wakeful. They had to go out into Palestine, and therefore were dressed as men ready for the journey, but you hope to go to heaven, and for this you must be ever watchful, for it is no slight torment that awaits the unworthy partaker. Think how odious to you is the traitor and those who crucified Jesus Christ! See then, that you be not yourself also guilty of the Body and Blood of Christ. They mangled His most holy Body, and you, after so

many and great benefits, receive Him with a defiled soul! For He considered it not enough to be made man, to be smitten on the cheek, and to be slain, but He even communicates to us His Own Self, and makes us, not through faith only, but truly and indeed to be His Body. Much more then must he be pure, who partakes of this sacrament. Truly, both the hands that divide this Body and the lips that are filled with this spiritual Fire and the tongue moistened with this most awesome Blood must be purer even than the rays of the sun. Think to what an honor you are admitted! What a table you enjoy! A table at the sight of which the very angels themselves tremble and dare not so much as look at it without fear, because of the rays of glory that break forth from it. And from this we are fed; of this we are partakers; and we become one body, one flesh with Christ. Who shall declare the wonders of the Lord, or show forth all His praise?

In his third moral on Ephesians, St John Chrysostom also says the following: "I see many who communicate of the Body of Christ perfunctorily, as it were by chance, out of custom and rule, rather than with reflection or thought. When the holy season of Lent comes, in whatever state a man may be, he communicates of the Mysteries, although, perchance, it is then not the right time for him to approach. For it is not Lent that makes men fit to approach, but holiness and purity of soul. With these, approach freely always and at all seasons; without these, never."[45]

Those who are not ready to be absolved after confession or those who have received absolution but have been told by their confessor to abstain from the Divine Communion until they overcome their evil habit and show fruits worthy of repentance are of course not to be admitted to partake of the Mysteries. Likewise, neither should persons out of their mind be allowed to commune, since they cannot examine themselves, which is absolutely required by the apostle (1 Cor 11:28). Furthermore, the priest must take care that when he gives the Communion of the Holy Mysteries to his people, he does not give any of the particles offered in commemoration of the Saints,

The Sacrament of Holy Communion 103

for the living, and for the dead but only the one oblation of the Lamb, which he himself has broken, for none of those other particles are the Body of Christ. Neither should he commune any with the water that is used to rinse the chalice after Communion, still less with the holy water blessed on Theophany. Some ignorant priests do this, thereby introducing a new Sacrament of their own, while others, either from ignorance or carelessness or through other circumstances, have dared to do the same not considering that they are guilty of grievous sin.

Of course, Holy Communion should not be considered outside of the context of the Divine Liturgy. The Liturgy is the most sublime work on earth, and the priest is called to perform it each time anew, for the entire essence of the Liturgy is not a repetition; it is a supreme newness, life itself being created again and again. It is not just a renewal but life-giving virgin soil. The living Christ, His saving sacrifice, and the participation of the priest and of the whole Church are not the Liturgy's breath of grace but its very heart. Deadness in a pastor can and must be conquered by one means alone: the love for Christ abiding in his heart. The clergyman must never grow accustomed to serving, that is, he must never perform the services, especially the Divine Liturgy, without fear, audaciously, as though it were any other secular affair.

The Cross of Christ is the strength of a pastor at all times and in everything. Recalling the Cross, carrying it in his heart and thoughts, implementing it in his life, living by the Cross, the pastor will be unassailable, and he will not consciously permit any diversion from the spiritual, salvific path. All the priest's actions, service, his entire cross-bearing path will then be salvific, clear, straight, and true.

The faithful arrive at the church. They see icons before them; all of heaven seems to appear in the iconostasis, and in the center, in the open royal doors stands the priest. Without him there is no service, no Sacrament, no grace issuing from the altar. Without him the church is dumb. He is a living icon in the iconostasis; by his service, by himself, he unites heaven and earth. Here he represents the Church and Christ Himself (especially if the clergyman is a bishop); he is the natural center of the service. Hence the importance of the question: What kind of person is the clergyman? Does he conform to his elevated office? Does he recognize fully his responsibility before God and the people of God? Does he possess the qualities of a Christian pastor, which make him a true pastor, and not a hireling, or still worse, a wolf among a herd of sheep?

In church, the priest opens up in all fullness. Here he is the performer of the mysteries, celebrant, caretaker of souls, provider. Here everything is significant: every movement, every exclamation; the whole appearance of the pastor is that of a father.

Sincerity gives birth to naturalness during services, but there must always also be a pious strictness so that the church does not become simply a place for personal feelings and emotions; a podium, a pedestal for the pastor; and so that the pastor himself, united with all in humility, might be a bearer of the spirit of the Church—a living and life-giving churchliness. For this, a pastor must have a fear of personal exaltation, a fear of becoming the object of cultish veneration in the church. It is important to have authority and the respect of one's parishioners and brothers, but priest-worship is always harmful to the Church and for the priest himself. The priest is called to always be a bearer of churchliness, of a lofty spiritual life, and of a profound Christian spirit.

Behind the iconostasis the priest stands before the altar table, which symbolizes in itself the immaterial throne of God Almighty. Therefore, conversation, jesting, excessive sitting, and quarreling are inappropriate. One must not be permitted to bring hats and outerwear into the altar. Naturally, spitting is inexcusable in church. The entire church should always be in exemplary order and cleanliness. And if there are no ancient icons, brocaded vestments, or elegant church ware, then the church may still be magnificent in its cleanliness, in its well thought-out, churchly appearance. This will always bear witness to the love of God in those who care for the beauty of the House of God.

A few more counsels regarding the upkeep of the church are in order here. The spiritual heart of the church is the altar. It is natural that here all must befit the holiness of the place. Perfect cleanliness, order, and absence of secular objects are absolutely required, as, of course, is appropriate behavior on the part of those people who are allowed to be in the altar. It is very good practice for there not to be any people in the altar who are not pertinent to the service being performed. A clergyman must be the first to show an example of how one must relate to the altar and conduct himself in it.

It is pleasant to see well-kept altars where everything is well thought-out and everything is lovingly positioned in its own place. Here even the air itself is clean. Here nothing is irrelevant. Everything is important, and everything together is a sure indicator of the people's regard for church's Holy of Holies. The part of the iconostasis inside the altar should not be thought of as its back side, where there can be dirt, cobwebs, and maybe even a mirror, but as the altar side, that is, the side facing toward the east, toward the altar table. It is very good when iconostases are made two-sided, with sacred icons or frescoes on the altar side as well.

The church's vestry is of no little importance. Its contents should correspond to the yearly cycle of services; here should be everything necessary for the performance of the Sacraments and services of need. Vessels, books, liturgical utensils—these are objects that are sacred, rare, beautiful, often old. These need to be cared for; their keeper needs to be mindful of their holiness and uniqueness. Treatment of holy objects is always a good indicator of a clergyman's faith and culture.

It happens that not enough attention is given to the book of Epistles—after the reading of the appointed section it is sometimes left wherever it happens to be set down. The sacred icons, antimins, holy chrism, Gospel, burial shroud, and holy crosses, demand special treatment by the priest. They must be in the church in proper condition, undamaged and whole, and they must be handled reverently, carefully, as sacred objects.

It is very important to store them in a fitting place. If restoration is in order, then they should be entrusted only to experienced restorers; otherwise, an old icon, embroidery, engraving, or enamel work can be ruined. Every clergyman is obligated to appreciate the artistic value of church objects, their antiquity, and to know their history. This is his direct responsibility.

It is essential to have icons for every day of the liturgical year, and all of them should be carefully kept. There are various methods for storing icons, vestments, books, and utensils. What is important is to prevent the damage and premature ruin of the treasures of every church's vestry.

Icons, embroidery, and vestments must never, for any reason, be rubbed with oil, scented water, or perfume; acid must not be used to clean silver. On aers, shrouds, vestments, inside *kamilavkas* (hats worn by clergy), and in general, wherever there is a lining, that lining should be clean. Covers and napkins should also be in impeccable condition. This to say nothing of the antimins. Every priest understands that the antimins on the altar of his church must be in order; it needs to have been blessed by an Orthodox bishop, contain relics, and be kept in proper cleanliness and neatness.

Dilapidated objects that are unfit for use should be burned in a separate place.

Old icons and things made from wood attract insects, so one needs to battle skillfully against these pests, these enemies of antiquities. Problems to be aware of include moths, dampness, nails, old icon plating, and, of course, disorderly storage, when icons lie in a pile, from which necessary ones are pulled as needed.

The majesty and sanctity of the church and services demand of the clergyman special attention toward movements in church. There should be something said here about the sign of the cross, blessings, bows and the raising of one's hands, censing, and walking. A clergyman must sign himself with the sign of the cross correctly, distinctly, and with reverence. Having signed himself with a full cross, he should make a bow, but not hastily and without throwing his head or hands about.

A clergyman must teach the faithful to make the sign of the cross correctly both by his word and by example. Signing the cross carelessly, incorrectly placed fingers, crossing oneself using two fingers or one's whole hand, or waving one's hand about immediately arouse feeling of revulsion and bear witness to the lack of reverence and fear of God in the person crossing himself. It is bad for a clergyman who has let his beard grow long to cross only his beard, not making the sign of the cross, as is proper, over his shoulders. Crossing one's mouth after yawning is a strange habit that ought to be discarded.

It is also important how a priest blesses those who approach him during services. Carelessness, rushing, and putting out one's hand to be kissed in a compulsory fashion also leave bitter traces in a person's soul. When blessing during a service, it is not necessary to raise one's hand higher than one's head. One must depict the cross clearly with correctly placed fingers and should always look at the person (or thing) whom (or which) he is blessing.

When blessing with the holy cross, one must not wave it about or lower it downwards. The cross is a sacred thing, and it is with an awareness of its greatness that one should bless the people with it and present it for veneration. It is inexcusable to wave the cross around while doing this.

Bows and prostrations should be made where appointed, and one must also see that they are made in a seemly fashion, fully in keeping with the reverent nature of the service. Arbitrary bows and kneeling where not appointed are unacceptable. At home, one may make any number of bows, but this should not be done in everyone's presence.

Censing is very difficult at first. Few know how to cense beautifully. One should cense in sets of three, making a bow with each. While censing, one must always look at the icon being censed. One must not hurry when censing, or wave the censer wildly about, or speak. One should cense with reverence and fear, never forgetting that this is a sacred action, an essential part of the service. Hurried censing during a molieben, at a panikhida, or at a burial gives a repulsive impression. Here, by the grave, standing with people who are deeply suffering, a priest must not rush, not just formally officiate and let that be the end. This is a crime!

A deep and meaningful celebration of the Liturgy is especially important. Everything in the Divine Liturgy has great significance, and there is nothing irrelevant, nothing secondary in it. One must feel the harmony of the Liturgy and its majesty, unveil it, and not impoverish it, not belittle the grandeur and fullness of the Divine Liturgy. When one lives the Liturgy, one can encourage the congregation to live it as well, and oftentimes the church and worshiping congregation inspire the priest. Everything in the Liturgy must be thought through with regard also to actions. Then the content and words will be accentuated by actions and movements. Everything in the Liturgy is important and sacred—from beginning to end.

I should like to mention some moments from the Liturgy—these are the clergy's kiss of peace before the Symbol of Faith during a celebration of several priests and the waving of the aer over the diskos and chalice during "I believe." These actions must be performed very conscientiously and reverently.

A bishop's presence in the altar at the Liturgy, as well as at other services, introduces certain peculiarities that all clergymen ought to know. First of all, the priest must receive a blessing from the bishop at the beginning and also he must remember to bow to the bishop following exclamations. When a bishop is present, a clergyman does not bless the other celebrants and the people. In this instance, at the Liturgy he blesses only the Holy Bread and Chalice during the Eucharistic Canon.

A hierarchical service has many peculiarities, and the clergy taking part in one ought to be especially attentive and composed. Often the Liturgy is greatly delayed due to reading the commemoration slips for the living and departed. This is very bad. The slips must be read, but not over too lengthy a period of time. It is not good if the Cherubic Hymn has to be repeated several times because the bishop is too long at the table of oblation, commemorating the living and departed.

During a service when several clergy are celebrating together, it is very important that general order be observed. All those serving should align themselves next to their senior, making the sign of the cross simultaneously with him, as well as bows and even readings from the service book. It is not a good practice to carry one's service book, which is sometimes quite bulky, inside one's belt during the Liturgy.

The behavior in the church and altar of clergy who are not serving is also revealing. Reading commemoration slips, cutting particles from *antidoron*, and other such activities absolutely must cease during the reading of the Gospel or during the Eucharistic Canon. It is discourteous not to listen during a brother's sermon or to criticize the content or manner of delivery. One must not sit in the altar in the presence of a bishop or those superior by ordination while they are standing. One must not sit in the altar during the time of communion. It is not good to rush in front of the serving priests to partake of the post-communion bread and wine.

The priest must also bring communion to the sick who are unable to attend the Divine Liturgy. It is his responsibility to take unremitting care that they depart not to the other world without the Communion of the Holy Mysteries, which is most necessary and salvific. To this end, he should admonish his parishioners that whenever they have anyone sick in their houses, they should give him notice immediately, and he, upon receiving such notice, should leave everything else and hasten to the sick person so that he may have time, while the mind is still clear, to bring him to true repentance. After hearing his confession, he may give him Communion worthily, and so, with that provision for the way, we may let him depart in hope of the resurrection and everlasting life. In the contrary case, if from any negligence on his part a sick man dies without having received Communion, the priest is to be subjected to a severe inquiry or even, under certain circumstances, to be suspended. Those who may have neglected to give notice to the priest are excluded from the Divine Mysteries.

St John Chrysostom in his sixth book *On the Priesthood* (ch. IV) has the following passage: "I was once told by a certain man—who heard it not from anyone else, but had been honored by God to see and hear the thing itself—that if any are departing this life and receive Communion with a pure conscience, then at the moment they expire, a multitude of Angels, attending the Holy Thing that they have received within them, surround, and conduct them from that place."

The same Father, in his third moral on Acts, says the following: "If even a single person departs without having received Communion, has not the priest entirely ruined his own salvation? For the loss of one soul is so great a thing that no words can describe it. For if its salvation is of so much worth that even the Son of God was made man and suffered all those sufferings for its sake, think what punishment and torment must await him who causes its loss."

CHAPTER 10

The Sacrament of Matrimony

Those who are about to enter into matrimony should be told by the priest to what purpose God ordained marriage, and they should be taught from this their duties to one another. Since God established marriage for the increase of mankind (Gen 1:28), and not merely so (for procreation is also common to beasts), but for the increase of mankind to glorify their Creator. This is also why man was created in the image and likeness of God (verse 27). Therefore, they who marry should consider the end and object of their union to be the procreation of children to be brought up in the fear of God, in His true faith, and in all manner of virtue.

Since God ordained matrimony for mutual help (Gen 2:18), the priest should also teach those who marry that they owe each to each faithfulness and help, the source of which is sincere love both in prosperity and in adversity, in health and in sickness, however disagreeable or tedious the sickness may be or whatever else may befall. He should teach that the wife must be subject to her husband as to the head and give him reverence while the husband must love the wife as his own body, even as himself. She is not his slave, and he must give her honor, as to the weaker vessel (1 Pet 3:5–7; Eph 5:22–33).

Furthermore, since marriage became a preventative remedy against fornication after man fell into sin and his carnal appetites ran wild, it follows that it is the duty of married persons even in matrimony itself to avoid fornication, that is, not only adultery with other persons but also every kind of excess (1 Cor 7:5, 29; 1 Thess 4:3–7). Their marriage must be not in word only but also in deed "honorable among all and the bed undefiled" (Heb 13:4; Eph 5:32). It may be profitable to read the history of the virtuous Tobias to prospective newlyweds, paying especial attention to the words: "I now am taking this kinswoman of mine, not because of lust, but with sincerity. Grant that she and I may find mercy and that we may grow old together" (Tob 8:7).

St John Chrysostom, in his twelfth moral on Colossians, says the following: "Marriage is a sacrament, and the image of a great thing, and even if you do not revere it for itself, yet revere that of which it is the symbol"—that is, the union of Christ the Son of God with His Church. "This is a great mystery, and I am applying it to Christ and the Church" (Eph 5:32).

The priest should further strictly charge them that their marriage should be celebrated decently in Christian, not in pagan, fashion without lewd and scandalous songs, without dances and cries that are found in pagan ceremonies. Also, let there be no divinations or any other kind of superstitious practice, for such practices are suggested by the evil spirit, and as is the seed sown, so also are the fruits that come of it. The spirit in which any marriage is celebrated will likely determine the future life of the newly married couple.

A week or more before celebrating any marriage, on a Sunday or feast day, the priest must give notice of it to the congregation in the Church (as is prescribed by the Nomocanon[46]) to prevent all unlawful marriages. He must ask if anyone knows of any lawful cause or impediment to the union of the parties in matrimony, and if so, bidding him to declare it. Meanwhile, it is the priest's duty to question the man and the woman whether they know the Lord's Prayer, the Creed, and the Ten Commandments, for it is shameful and sinful to enter the marriage state and to become the father and mother of children without knowing that which will be their duty to teach their children. Further, the priest must be sure to know the degrees of consanguinity within which the canons of the Church forbid marriage, and if in any case he is in doubt, he must seek the advice of his bishop.

The priest is required to solemnize all marriages in the church building, in the presence of others as necessary witnesses. When the contract is to be made, he must ask both parties separately whether they wish of their own freewill to be married and without an answer to this question he must proceed no further. Should any person especially the young woman indicate that she does not consent, or that compulsion has been used, the priest should immediately break off the ceremony and admonish the parties attempting compulsion, since in these cases the marriage is not valid. In fact, whoever is guilty of such compulsion will be liable to be held guilty and punished, just as if he had been guilty of a forcible abduction.[47] It is forbidden under heavy penalties for parents to force their children into any marriage against their will.

A priest must be acquainted with the laws of his state and/or country concerning the legal age to marry and whether parental consent is needed in cases of underage marriage. He should also not marry very old people, or such that are mutilated or otherwise unfit for the duties of marriage, nor any out of their minds, or intoxicated (until they are sober), nor any who do not know the Ten Commandments and the essential articles of the faith until they have learned them. Canon XI of Timothy, Archbishop of Alexandria, has these words: "If a priest, after having been called upon to solemnize a marriage, finds out that it is unlawful, let him not make himself partaker of other men's sins." Otherwise, the priest who marries any such couple is held by the canons to become a party to the offence of those who contract together unlawfully, and he subjects himself to canonical sanction.

Here it is proper for us to mention that the priest must on no account, without the knowledge and consent of his bishop, marry any Orthodox person to a person of another faith, even if that person is a Christian. In general, on the subject of mixed marriages between Orthodox persons and those of other faiths, a priest should always consult his bishop.

CHAPTER 11

The Sacrament of Unction

In this, as with other Sacraments, the priest should teach the person who needs the Sacrament of Unction with holy oil, if received with faith and sure trust in Christ Jesus, thus granting the healing of bodily disease and the forgiveness of sins that may have been committed, according to the General Epistle of the Apostle James, chapter 5, verses 14 through 15. However, since forgiveness of sins and a living and salvific faith in Christ Jesus require and imply true repentance, the sick person must by all means, before being anointed, prepare himself by true repentance, confess his sins, and receive absolution.

The priest should also exhort the sick person to give his life into the Lord's hands and to think of what is to come: of how he must appear before God, the Judge of all men. Here let him never take his mind's eye off from Jesus Christ, our Mediator with God, and our Salvation, Who alone is "the atoning sacrifice for our, and ... for the sins of the whole world" (1 John 2: 2), Who "was handed over to death for our trespasses and was raised for our justification" (Rom 4:25), and to Him alone let him cling with all his heart and hold Him, like the Patriarch Jacob of old, saying, "I will not let You go unless You bless me" (Gen 32:26).

Indeed it is the priest's duty at all times during sickness, and not only when unction is administered but especially on the approach of death, to keep up the despondent heart of the sick and to comfort his troubled soul by visiting him expressly for that purpose, by giving him from God's word such instruction and consolation as may best strengthen him and send him forth on his journey, and to help him pass from this temporal life to the life eternal in hope of salvation. The last hours of a man's life and the moments of the agony of death especially demand this.

On such occasions we may use the following:

1. Psalms such as those numbered 23, 27, 42, 116, 142, and the Penitential Psalms, 6, 38, 51, 130, and 141.

2. From the other books of the infallible word of God, we should choose those passages in which it is clearly shown that God does not will the death of a sinner but is willing to save all: "As I live thus says the Lord: 'I do not will the death of the ungodly man. So the ungodly man should, turn from his way and live'" (Ezek 33:11). The same is confirmed in 1 Timothy chapter 2, verse 4. Also, we should set forth God's love to mankind, reminding the dying person that God sent His Son into the world to save sinners: "For God so loved the world that He gave His Own only begotten Son, that whoever believes in Him should not perish but have everlasting life" (John 3:16). "But go and learn what this means: 'I desire mercy and not sacrifice.' For I did not come to call the righteous, but sinners, to repentance" (Matt 9:13). And the holy Apostle Paul writes: "If God is for us, who can be against us? He who did not spare His own Son, but delivered Him up for us all, how shall He not with Him also freely give us all things?" (Rom 8:31–32).

3. Again, we should use those texts that assure us that the sinner who repents is justified solely by God's grace, through living and saving faith, and by nothing else whatsoever. "Being justified freely through His grace through the redemption that is in Christ Jesus, whom God set forth as a propitiation by His blood, through faith" (Rom 3:24–25). "For by grace you have been saved through faith, and that not of yourselves; it is the gift of God, not of works, lest anyone should boast" (Eph 2:8–9). The Blood of Jesus Christ (that is, through true repentance and trust in Him) "cleanses us from all sin" (1 John 1:7). See also Hebrews chapter 10, verse 19.

4. Furthermore, we should assure the sick that this goodness of God is not to be overcome by any amount of transgressions. All that

is required is for the sinner truly and sincerely to repent. For our heavenly Father most lovingly receives all repentant sinners, as we may show by the examples of the prodigal son (Luke 15:11), the tax collector (Luke 18:9), the thief on the cross (Luke 23:42), David who had committed adultery and murder (2 Sam 12:11–13), Peter who apostatized (Luke 22:61), and the sinful woman who repented (Luke 7:38).

5. When we set forth the love of God, we may read chapter 17 of John's Gospel and chapter 15 of First Corinthians and suggest to the sick that temporal death is only a sleep and a passage from this troublesome life straight to everlasting bliss to those who truly repent, believe, and trust in Jesus Christ (John 5:24).

6. All who believe in Christ and die trusting in Him shall rise again at the last day (John 6:40) not to condemnation but to the inheritance of the kingdom of heaven and to everlasting glory (Phil 3:20–21).

PART III

On Prayer

CHAPTER 12

On Prayer in General

The word of God directs us to pray to the Lord, and natural reason—when in a sound state—leads man to do the same, for there is one God, the sole Author and Provider of everything good. Whatever good, beauty, or strength that creatures possess, they receive it all from His fullness, and He distributes all His mercies and bounties solely by His own almighty goodness and wisdom, according to His will: "A man can receive nothing unless it has been given to him from heaven" (John 3:27). "Every good gift and every perfect gift is from above, and comes down from the Father of lights" (James 1:17).

But since man needs to be prepared and enabled to receive those manifold mercies and bounties that God distributes, the Lord Himself gives us, as His reasonable creatures, one especial means, which is the command to pray: "Ask, and it will be given you; seek, and you will find; knock, and it will be opened to you" (Matt 7:7). "Ask, and you will receive" (John 16:24). And for the fulfillment of this commandment, He has also prescribed to us a specific form of prayer, the "Our Father" (Matt 6:9).

However, it was not for His own sake that He gave us this law but for ours, so that we, knowing Him alone to be both our life and the giver of everything good, might not seek other gods to fulfill our wants and necessities or make gods of any of the creatures, as in former times was done by the pagans who did not know God. Instead, through prayer we can ask Him for everything good and profitable for us, since He is our Maker and Lord.

The Lord was pleased to ordain this way and order for man and so to distinguish him in the reception and use of His benefits from all other creatures. Thus, it seemed good to His unsearchable wisdom and goodness to the end that man receiving good gifts from the right hand of the Most High should use them not as the beasts that have no understanding but as a reasonable creature with prayer and thanksgiving, glorifying His most holy Name.

It is clear that prayer is the means given by God to man by help of which he may draw near in mind to God and devoutly present himself to ask good gifts of Him, and whatever he asks according to His will with faith, in spirit, and in truth, God will give him. To be brief: prayer is the ascent or lifting up of our mind to God to ask Him for good gifts. Or in other words: prayer is asking God for good gifts with devotion.

Here we must understand that under the general name "prayer" many different duties or parts of the service of God, both inward and outward, are included. Christ said the following: "The true worshippers will worship the Father in spirit and truth" (John 4:23), and concerning love for God: "You shall love the Lord your God with all your heart, with all your soul, and with all your mind" (Matt 22:37). The apostle said, "Present your bodies a living sacrifice, holy, acceptable to God, which is your reasonable service" (Rom 12:1). All these and similar commandments are practiced and fulfilled only with true prayer.

The duties belonging to the inward service of God are these: true knowledge of God and of His law, faith in our Lord Jesus Christ, love for God and our neighbor, trust in God, fear of God, purity of heart, humility, obedience, meekness, patience, and constant thankfulness. All these duties spring from one root. In other words, from the true knowledge of God and His will spring faith and love and from these all the rest. This makes them all so bound together that not one of them can exist in any perfection without the rest. But true prayer in its essence embraces all these different parts and so includes and implies them in its own name, nor indeed without them can it itself exist.

The above-named duties are great virtues and produce marvelous effects in man. Faith brings him to God; love unites him and makes him one spirit with the Lord (1 Cor 6:17); trust or hope comforts him; the fear of God makes him wise to salvation and never allows him to depart from God; purity enlightens him; humility and obedience with repentance give him remission of sins; patience and meekness make him strong and unwavering in all his duties; thankfulness helps him love his Benefactor, but the only way to attain all these is prayer.

From the inward service of God should proceed the outward, for the outward service of God ought to be nothing else than the manifestation of the inward for the glory and praise of the Most High. These duties include the following: confession of our most holy faith, the preaching of God's word on Sundays and feast days, going to church for public prayer, hearing the reading, singing, and especially the word of God read and preached, giving alms to the poor and doing all manner of good deeds for the needs of our neighbors, building or furnishing churches, as well as making particular offerings or gifts for such ends. All these things are sacrifices well pleasing to God (Heb 13:16) if they proceed directly from the inward worship or service, that is, from faith and love for God and neighbor.

Natural reason—in its sound state—has some idea of this latter kind of worship, as well as the former, either innate or derived from contemplation of creation: "The heavens declare the glory of God ... and night unto night showeth knowledge" (Ps 18:2–3 LXX). However, for the conception of such outward service of God to be sound and complete, and for all its realization in practice to be free from superstition, one needs something more than mere natural revelation, for which reason we establish our worship on the writings of the apostles and prophets for their words are the words of God Himself, "confirmed for ever and ever, done in truth and equity" (Ps 110:8).

Prayer is divided into public, that is, ecclesiastical, and private. Public prayer is offered with the congregation in the church or in any other place where a number of believers are present; private prayer is that which an individual offers alone.

Private prayer is made in two ways:

1. When anyone in his house, or elsewhere, retires from company and prays privately to the Lord. Concerning this kind of private prayer, the Lord said: "Go into your room, and when you have shut your door, pray to your Father who is in the secret place; and your Father who sees in secret will reward you openly" (Matt 6:6).

2. When anyone, either in company or alone, sitting or standing, prays earnestly within his secret soul, not in words but in thought, with all his heart, all his strength, and all his mind, as standing before God Who is omnipresent. Concerning such prayer, the Apostle Paul says: "We ourselves groan within ourselves, eagerly waiting for the adoption, the redemption of our body" (Rom 8:23), and in another place: "singing with grace in your hearts to the Lord" (Col 3:16). "By night I communed with mine own heart, and searched my soul" (Ps 76:7). Concerning prayer in general, both private and public, Christ said: "The true worshippers will worship the Father in spirit and truth" (John 4:23–24), and His apostle said: "I will pray with the spirit, and I will also pray with the understanding" (1 Cor 14:15).

An example of the first kind of private prayer was given to us by Christ Himself: Jesus "went up on the mountain by Himself to pray" (Matt 14:23). "He Himself often withdrew into the wilderness and prayed" (Luke 5:16). He "continued all night in prayer to God" (Luke 6:12).

Examples of the second kind of private prayer include the following: Moses at the Red Sea, when he encouraged the children of Israel and exhorted them to trust in the Lord, made no prayer with his lips, but he called upon God with his heart only and was heard: "Why do you cry to Me?" (Exod 14:15). Another excellent example is Hannah, the mother of the Prophet Samuel: "as [Hannah] spoke in her heart ... her voice was not heard." She explained: "I pour out my soul before the Lord" (1 Kgs 1:13,15 LXX). (On the same subject, see also Nehemiah 2:4.)

Private prayer, when made in the first way, is called oral or outward, but when made in the second, it is called inward or mental. This latter by itself, even without the oral, is well pleasing to God and profitable to the soul that prays, as the examples and commandments cited above show us. But outward and oral prayer, if it is without the inward, is of no value. Not only that, but if a person prays like a hypocrite willingly—meaning through hypocrisy and not through mere natural infirmity—it is abomination in the sight of the Lord, even dangerous to the soul of him that prays for his prayer is turned into sin (Matt 6:5; Luke 18:11).

The inward prayer of the heart can at all times be offered up in thought, by the spirit, and with faith. Therefore, the devout man who fears God can pray everywhere and constantly; indeed, he is bound to do so, according to the command of the apostle: "praying always with all prayer and supplication in the Spirit" (Eph 6:18). In fact, nothing can hinder him (Rom 8:35) if only he is zealous toward God and has a constant sense of His presence. For, in such a state of spirit, what can hinder a man from saying in his heart, "Have mercy on me, O God! God help me!" and other such prayers?

Yet, although spiritual prayer without oral is efficacious, while oral without spiritual can never be so, one can by no means limit oneself to mental or inward prayer and neglect oral prayer. Man is a being of both soul and body; therefore, he must pray and give glory to God with his body as well as his spirit (1 Cor 6:20). Therefore, holy David exclaims: "Hear my words, O Lord; consider my cry. Attend to the voice of my supplication, my King and my God" (Ps 5:2). And our Lord, when He taught His disciples to pray, said the following: "When you pray, say: Our Father … " (Luke 11:2). Both the Lord and David are speaking of prayer with the lips and body without excluding what is inward and spiritual, and this truth is most strongly established both by the examples left us of our Saviour Himself (John 17; Matt 26:39–42), the Apostles (Acts 1:24 and 4:24), the prophets, and by the Psalms of David. Therefore, since we ought to pray in our hearts always, we should also pray with our lips at the appointed times, as well as with our hearts.

But to prevent oral prayer (both public and private) from becoming a sin, lest Christians become guilty of the following condemnation: "This people draw near to Me with their mouth, and honor Me with their lips, but their heart is far from Me" (Matt 15:8). We must strive and labor with all our souls to precede and accompany our oral prayer always with inward prayer of the heart and never at any time separate the two.

This we may do in the following way: when we prepare our bodies for prayer, we should also prepare and present our whole soul to the Lord. When we bend our knees, we should bend with them the knees of the heart; when we raise our hands and lift up our eyes on high, we should also lift up all the thoughts of our hearts, as it is written: "Let us lift our hearts and our hands to the Most High in heaven" (Lam 3:37 LXX). Finally, when we say with our lips, "Have mercy on me, O God," we should cry out these same words with our whole heart and so the words of our lips and the meditation of our heart will be equally acceptable in the sight of the Lord (Ps 18:15).

Both public and private prayer, therefore, must always be offered in spirit and in truth, and our Heavenly Father Himself expects this of us (John 4:23). But what do these words—*in spirit* and *in truth*—actually mean? According to the Fathers, to pray in spirit is to pray with faith, fear, and love for God, and with the deepest humility and contrition of heart; to pray in truth is to pray with attention and with the understanding, neither insincerely nor only outwardly.

This can easily help anyone examine his own prayer, whether it is in spirit and truth or only with the lips. If anyone does not sense in his heart a movement of devotion toward God, that is, if he does not have fear and love, then he does not pray in spirit; moreover, if he is not attentive during his prayers, then neither does he pray in truth. Thus, every person should watch himself, and if he finds himself lacking in true prayer, he will be able easily, with the aid of God's grace, to correct the fault.

All those who pray merely with the body sin against the commandments of the Gospel. These include those who pray by speaking

much, or with frequent repetition, or in mere outward bows, kneeling, or prostrations, without having at the same time any warmth
toward God or even without seeking to have any. Such people say
one thing, but think another. Still more do those people sin who pray
hypocritically, merely to appear before others to pray, but do not have
God in their thoughts. Therefore, all these must, for the amendment
of their prayers, keep in their memory the following rule: "God is
Spirit, and those who worship Him must worship in spirit and truth"
(John 4:24).

CHAPTER 13

How to Pray in Spirit and Truth

When we are about to approach God, either in public or in private, and are preparing to call upon His wonderful and holy Name, let us reflect on His tremendous majesty and His unsearchable omnipresence. Let us also reflect on our own vileness and spiritual poverty, considering Who is our God and who we are ourselves. He is Spirit, immortal, all-pure, all-good, seeing through our inmost soul and thoughts; but we are clothed with flesh, mortal, evil, and in our thoughts unclean in His sight. Therefore, we must purify ourselves from all filthiness of the flesh and spirit, and so with all possible devotion and awe call upon His Name, "For our God is a consuming fire" (Heb 12:29) and His Name is great, terrible, and holy (Ps 98:3).

As may be concluded from the above, if our God is an all-pure Spirit and His Name is wonderful and holy, then everyone who prays should diligently contemplate God, remembering that He is so holy and just that He cannot endure even the slightest impurity or unrighteousness: "Thou art a God that hast no pleasure in wickedness" (Ps 5:5). We must also contemplate ourselves to examine whether we are truly and sincerely repentant for our sins and repent before the Lord. Or do we instead sin over and over again without ceasing? For God does not heed impenitent sinners (John 9:31). The blood-thirsty and deceitful man the Lord abhors, but if anyone is a true worshipper of God, he must flee to God with all his soul and be sorry for his sins and begin to do God's will, and God will hear him. Finally, we should reflect also on what we ask of God and make sure that it is not contrary to His will, or these words will apply to us: "You do not know what you ask" (Mark 10:38).

Besides the above reflections, all of us must have the following intentions: to render by our prayer due honor to God: "Bring unto the

Lord, O ye sons of God ... glory and honor" (Ps 28:1 LXX), to excite such emotions in our hearts and preserve such dispositions of spirit, as are fitting from us lowly ones to the Divine Majesty and Holiness (2 Cor 7:1; 1 Pet 1:16), to testify from a pure heart our true Gospel faith, sincere hope, and ardent love for God (Mark 12:30), to lay before God the wishes of our heart, or our petitions for good gifts, with the profoundest humility and devotion (Luke 18:13; Matt 8:9). But with all this, we must not trust in ourselves, nor in our prayers, but solely in our Lord Jesus Christ and in His mercy, "For all the promises of God in Him are Yes, and in Him Amen, to the glory of God through us" (2 Cor 1:20).

Our God is so very merciful, long-suffering, and of such great goodness that He is more ready to stretch out His hands to give than we are to receive, every day and hour pouring out upon us His bounties, giving us breath, life, and all things profitable for the enjoyment of life (1 Tim 6:17) and delivering us from all evil. Therefore, who is there who can consider and weigh these great benefits without having his whole heart and soul stirred up to pray to God? Holy David, meditating on this from the depth of his soul, cries out: "Bless the Lord O my soul, and all that is within me bless His holy Name. Bless the Lord O my soul, and forget not all His benefits" (Ps 102:1–2 LXX).

The thought of God's inconceivable love is a powerful assistance to pray in spirit and in truth: "God so loved the world that He gave His only begotten Son" for us (John 3:16). This love inflamed the Apostle Paul when he said of himself and of all others like him: "Who shall separate us from the love of Christ? Shall tribulation, or distress, or persecution, or nakedness, or peril, or sword?" (Rom 8:35) No, nothing. But looking to Jesus, Who suffered for us, and seeing the love of God, which surpasses all understanding, the Apostle Paul prays in spirit and in truth, seeking to teach us also to do the same: "For this reason I bow my knees to the Father of our Lord Jesus Christ ... that He would grant you ... to know the love of Christ which passes knowledge; that you may be filled with all the fullness of God" (Eph 3:14,16,19).

Whoever in a similar manner will look with all his soul to our Lord Jesus Christ, Who suffered for us, and consider His sufferings, His death, burial, and resurrection, in which, as in a painting, he sees his own justification represented most vividly, he will certainly pray with all his heart and mind. For his heart will then be so touched by Christ's love that he will almost forget himself, and he will rise to such a pitch in prayer that he will pray now no longer with words but with tears, as St Basil and St Augustine say, not with breath but rather with sighs. What his heart will then feel and his soul will see, his tongue will not be able to express. This is how absorbed holy David was when he cried: "For what have I in heaven, and what have I desired upon earth from Thee? My flesh and my heart have failed ... " (Ps 72:25–26 LXX). And the Apostle Paul, smitten with the arrow of this same love, says: "For I am persuaded that neither death nor life, nor angels ... nor any other created thing, shall be able to separate us from the love of God which is in Christ Jesus our Lord" (Rom 8:38–39).

Great assistance to true prayer will be found in God's promises, if we truly and firmly believe them. Through them faith in the Gospel is increased in men, love grows, and hope is established immovable. Examples of this we have in Abraham (Rom 4:20–21) and others (Heb 11:2). By this means a man is stirred up to true prayer. For the very relation between the promises and their accomplishment leads to this, since there is no other way by which we can obtain the accomplishment of God's promises, except by true prayer.

Because of natural infirmity and other circumstances, a person's spirit is sometimes so weak and deficient, and his heart so cold, that he cannot bring himself to take the above-mentioned steps to aid his prayer, nor can he even think of God's mercy, love, and promises. He requires something special to stir up and improve his heart. Under such circumstances, we must force ourselves to pray out loud, even if our heart refuses, recalling to mind Christ's words: "The kingdom of heaven suffers violence, and the violent take it by force" (Matt 11:12); "Strive to enter through the narrow gate, for many will seek to enter and will not be able" (Luke 13:24). To aid us in meditating on these words of Christ, we may use as a prayer the words of David: "My soul cleaveth to the dust; O give me life, according to Thy word. My soul nodded off in weariness; sustain Thou me in Thy words. Take from me the way of injustice, and by Thy law have mercy upon me" (Ps 118:25,28,29 LXX). "Thou shalt quicken us, and we shall call upon Thy Name" (Ps 79:19 LXX). By this kind of compulsion a man will through oral prayer progress to inward prayer, and he will begin to pray in spirit and in truth, and so the one assists the other, with the cooperation of the Holy Spirit.

St Macarius, in the third chapter of his discourse *On Keeping the Heart*, writes the following: "Everyone must do his utmost to force himself to abide continually in prayer, always begging and expecting the Lord to come and make His abode within him, and to teach and confirm him in all His commandments, so that his soul may become the temple of Jesus Christ." Further on in the same chapter, he writes: "And so God, seeing him striving, and forcibly compelling himself to what is good—even though his heart is reluctant—gives him the grace of true prayer."

St Augustine, in the fifth chapter of his treatise *On the Departed*, has these words: "Outward and oral prayer cannot be true without that which is inward, and even inward prayer of the heart fails without the oral, and dies away; but when joined with oral prayer, it increases and waxes more earnest."

Therefore, oral prayer especially leads him who prays to inward prayer of the heart when he attends devoutly and with faith to the words of his prayer, for the sense that lies in the words and the power of the spirit within them stir up our hearts and souls. He who prays will then begin to pray in spirit and in truth. In order to attain this kind of prayer, we should be careful to utter the words of our prayer not too rapidly, according to the injunction in Holy Scripture: "Do not be hasty with your mouth, and do not let your heart be quick to utter a word before God" (Eccl 5:1 LXX).

Reflection on past sins and the sense of God's anger against us for them, with the recollection of the terrible judgment and the thought of the punishment to come, is no slight assistance to prayer, for all these things very powerfully move man's heart and drive him to ask mercy of God. Such was the meditation of holy David, when he turned to the Lord and cried: "O Lord, rebuke me not in Thine anger, neither chasten me in Thy wrath ... O Lord, heal me, for my bones are vexed. My soul also is sore troubled" (Ps 6:1–4).

The help of the Spirit of God is the chief and most potent aid to prayer. For the Holy Spirit, as the apostle preaches, "helps in our weaknesses. For we do not know what we should pray for as we ought, but the Spirit Himself makes intercession for us with groanings which cannot be uttered" (Rom 8:26). And so, with this teacher and guide, all the above-mentioned meditations will be profitable and forceful, and the Spirit of God will Himself cooperate with us, directing and preparing our hearts to pray as we ought (Ezek 36:26). Therefore, all who pray should ask the Lord to send His Holy Spirit that He may teach us true prayer; for ourselves, we should give diligent heed with all our soul that we neither by deed, nor word, nor thought offend the Holy Spirit and so grieve Him, remembering the injunction given us: "And do not grieve the Holy Spirit of God, by whom ye were sealed for the day of redemption" (Eph 4:30).

Our God is everywhere present and fills all things; His name is great, awesome, and holy; and prayers offered in spirit and in truth are accepted by Him. Therefore, we who are mortal and sinful, when we draw near the throne of the Divine Majesty and call upon Him, we must lay aside all earthly thoughts. We must remember that we are standing before His face, and He is looking through our hearts. We must fall down devoutly on our face to the ground before the Almighty and All-merciful Maker and Saviour and give to Him honor and glory. We must testify to Him our faith and love, due to Him alone; we must confess our own unworthiness and wretchedness, like Manasseh, like the Publican, and the Prodigal son; and then, for the sake of His holy Name, we will ask Him to bestow on us His good gifts.

The good gifts of God are twofold: spiritual and temporal. Spiritual gifts include the following: knowledge of God, understanding of His law, faith in Christ Jesus, repentance, remission of sins, and others. Temporal gifts include health of body, food, drink, and clothing, all of which are strictly necessary. Gifts that are not necessary for our life include riches, honor, glory, and length of days.

The Lord's Prayer itself teaches us that we should ask for the above-mentioned good gifts from God. That prayer is both to all generally and to each one of us personally a perfect rule and lesson in how to pray, for it prescribes prayer for blessings both spiritual and temporal, and it mentions by name what those blessings are.

Here it will be profitable to say something of the Lord's Prayer. It is brief indeed, but yet in its brevity it takes in all necessary petitions that refer to man's life either in time or in eternity.

Our Saviour Jesus Christ, in the Prayer that He gave us (Luke 11:2–4), has prescribed the following:

1. That, before every thing else, we ask of our heavenly Father that His Name be sanctified: "Hallowed be Thy Name." God's Name is indeed holy in itself and the source of holiness, but in this petition we pray that He would be pleased to teach us to hallow His wonderful and holy Name, that is, know, love, invoke, and glorify It. Now God's Name is hallowed and honored in us—and we are sanctified in Him and by Him—when we know Him from His works, when we confess Him to be eternal, almighty, all-wise, all-good, just, and very merciful; when we admire His wonders and His unsearchable providence over ourselves and most sensibly acknowledge Him as the sole Author and Provider of all the good, spiritual and temporal that we enjoy in this life; when we give Him thanks, praising Him and saying, *"Holy, Holy, Holy, Lord God of Sabaoth ... "*[48]; when, with all this, we regulate our thoughts and works, and our life itself, to the honor and glory of His Name.

    But since we are unable thus to hallow God's Name by ourselves, we are directed to add a second petition—a means to this end—asking God for *His Kingdom.*

2. "Thy kingdom come." The kingdom of God "is an everlasting kingdom, and [His] dominion endureth throughout all ages" (Ps 144:13 LXX), but we here ask not this kingdom, but the kingdom

of grace and love (Col 1:13) and the kingdom of glory, that is, we ask Him to reign in us by the true faith of the Gospel, that the sin of unbelief may have no place in us, that the Holy Spirit may guide us into all truth (John 16:13), producing in us spiritual fruits (Gal 5:22), that our evil propensities may not have dominion over us (Rom 6:14), that the Lord keep from us also a life of transgression, and grant us instead that the kingdom of His grace grow in us day by day, both by a life lived according to the Gospel and faith. We also ask Him, after this mortal life, to make us inheritors of His everlasting kingdom of glory in Heaven.

But since neither can this kingdom of grace be established in us nor the brightness of His glory enlighten our hearts, until the darkness of sloth and the veil of disobedience is taken away from our souls (2 Cor 3:16) and until we become obedient to the Lord in all things, for this reason we are directed to ask our heavenly Father to give us the gift of obedience, that is, that He would put into our hearts the desire and the power to do His will.

3. And so by these words, "Thy will be done on earth as it is in heaven," we ask our Father, not that He should do what He wills, but that we may be enabled to do what He wills for us. But what He wills is this: He wants us all to "be saved and to come to the knowledge of the truth" (1 Tim 2:4), to hear His word, and believe in Him (John 6:29), and to do His will, which will lead us along the path of everlasting salvation. By this means given from God, the kingdom of grace is established in us, and by the grace of the Holy Spirit reigning in us we can easily hallow God's Name. Therefore, as the Apostle Peter says, "an entrance will be supplied to you abundantly into the everlasting kingdom of our Lord and Savior Jesus Christ" (2 Pet 1:11).

But to prevent us from being hindered from seeking heavenly spiritual gifts by the need of temporal good things, and so that we can lead our mortal life under the shelter of God's goodness, in tranquility, we are directed to add to our petitions for those other blessings one for temporal good things.

4. "Give us this day our daily bread." In this petition *bread* means everything needful and profitable, everything without which human life and society cannot continue. This includes all sciences, arts, branches of industry, and governments themselves, which serve to the well-being of human society. And though the Lord in His mercy, even without our asking, gives to all breath, and life, and "food in due season" (Ps 144:15 LXX) and appointed in nations the governing authorities (Rom 13:1), and through them implants sciences and arts (Dan 2:21; Prov 8:14), in His righteous judgments, in order to punish men for their ingratitude and iniquity, takes away these good things (Isa 3:1–3). Therefore, in this petition we ask Him to give us all things needful and profitable for this present life day by day, that is, we ask Him to give us temperate seasons and the increase of the fruits of the earth, to bless our labors and industry, and to keep us in health and strength of body, thereby ensuring the welfare of the whole community. And not only do we ask Him for this, but we imply at the same time, and with the same words, the further prayer that we may be enabled to use all these blessings to good, to His glory, and to the sanctification of His Name.

   But since we have a great hindrance to the attainment of temporal and spiritual good things in our sinfulness (for through our sins we are often deprived of every good), we are directed to ask of God pardon and remission of sins.

5. "Forgive us our debts, as we forgive our debtors." This petition leads us to repentance of all that we have done amiss. And since our Lord is very good and loves us, He cannot but desire that we also should in this imitate Him. Therefore, He lets us understand that our debts are forgiven when we also ourselves forgive our debtors (Matt 6:14–15). Therefore, we ought, as the apostle teaches us, to "be imitators of God as dear children" (Eph 5:1) and to "be kind one to another, tenderhearted, forgiving one another" even as we also desire to obtain forgiveness from God (Eph 4:32). In this way, and by this petition, Christ teaches us how to rid ourselves of our first and greatest hindrance.

6. There are, however, hindrances other than sin alone, particularly all temptations and scandals, inward and outward, of the flesh, the world, and the devil, by which man, either through the senses or without the senses, is enticed to sin. And so, the temptations that we have named draw us away from God's will and His kingdom, keeping us from hallowing His Name. And since we are unable with our own strength to stand against them and repel them, we are directed in the sixth and seventh petitions of the Lord's Prayer to ask deliverance and protection from all temptation, from every evil work, and also from our invisible enemy, the devil, who is always seeking to devour us. "Lead us not into temptation, but deliver us from the evil one."

7. The preface and conclusion of the Lord's Prayer contain what is intended to comfort us and to incite and confirm in us a good hope. The preface—"Our Father, Who art in Heaven"—sets before us the inconceivable mercy of God, which has vouchsafed to make us, unworthy as we are, His children (John 1:12) and heirs of His everlasting good things in Heaven (Rom 8:17). The conclusion—"For Thine is the kingdom, the power, and the glory, for ever and ever, Amen"—is replete with the strongest encouragement and immortal hope, since our Father is the sole Lord of heaven and earth, everlasting, and almighty. His is the kingdom, His the power, His the glory, for ever; therefore, if we call upon Him with faith and love, and if by our obedience we give Him honor and glory, then nothing will snatch us of His hand, and He will give unto us eternal life (John 10:28–29).

This prayer should be the more revered because the Lord Himself has given it to us, and in brief but wonderful order He included in it all petitions that are necessary for us. Therefore, it is the duty of all, without exception, to learn it and labor to understand it, and to pray it with the deepest devotion not only every evening and morning, on rising up and lying down, but at all times and on all occasions. This is required of us by those words of Christ: "When you pray, pray thus."

There are also other prayers written in Holy Scripture for both our instruction and use, such as the prayer of the publican: "God be merciful to me a sinner!" (Luke 18:13), the prayer of the prodigal son: "Father, I have sinned against heaven and in your sight" (Luke 15:21), and the prayer of the thief on the cross: "Lord, remember me, when You come into Your kingdom!" (Luke 23:42). These short prayers are for our use, and we should use them when asking God to pardon our sins.

Other than the Lord's Prayer and these others, it is not contrary to the Lord's will, but agreeable to Him, to ask God's mercy, whether for ourselves or for our brethren, in any such words as the circumstances and necessities of the case itself may suggest. We have many examples to teach us, such as the ten lepers who sought to be cleansed (Luke 17:13), the centurion who wished that his servant should be healed (Matt 8:8), and many others. All these used their own words, and only words suitable for their needs; and every one of them obtained what he sought. Whatever any person's necessity may be, he should not look about for many words but should call upon the Lord with words that the case itself and the warmth of his heart inspire in him.

It has been clearly enough shown above that we ought to ask both spiritual and temporal goods from God, but we must understand that spiritual good things are necessary and profitable to man for both this temporal life and the eternal, for they have the "promise of the life that now is and of that which is to come" (1 Tim 4:8), while bodily or temporal goods are profitable only for this present life. Therefore, we should undoubtedly desire and ask spiritual blessings at all times, but we should ask temporal and bodily blessings only if it will please our Lord and will not damage us and will serve to glorify His Name.

If anyone asks anything diligently from the Lord, but the Lord does not immediately answer the petition, he should not grow despondent. Instead, he should consider what it is that he asks: Is it a temporal or a spiritual benefit? If it is spiritual and necessary for salvation, let him unceasingly continue to ask with faith and patience, and it will be given him. But if it is anything temporal, let him not complain against the Lord, but resign himself to His will and providence, for we cannot foresee the future to know whether what we ask will be for our good or for our harm. But the Lord, Who is omniscient and all-wise, foresees all things (Ps 138:2–3 LXX) and, being good and merciful, He in His goodness does not give us what is harmful. Therefore, when we do not receive what we wish, we should not be upset, but instead we should give God thanks that He does not indulge us when it is harmful for us.

Nor should we in such cases think that our prayers are in vain if they were offered in spirit and truth, for the Lord mercifully hears us and accepts them, but instead of temporal blessings gives us spiritual ones; and if not in the present, yet in the world to come He repays us abundantly (Rom 2:6–7). For He is a just and merciful Judge; therefore, to all who call upon Him in truth He gives a crown of righteousness in the last day (2 Tim 4:8).

When we pray, we should add to our prayers our own diligence and patience. That is to say, he who prays to the Lord for any good thing should himself also at the same time labor for its accomplishment, using all proper means and avoiding all obstacles; at the same time, he should have patience to abide constantly in his labor and diligence, no less than in his prayers. And watchful and unremitting continuance in this is what both the Gospel commands (Luke 12:37; Col 4:2; 1 Thess 5:17) and man's nature itself absolutely requires. For man has become *carnal* since the fall, "sold under sin. For what I am doing, I do not understand. For what I will do, that I do not practice; but what I hate, that I do" (Rom 7:14–15). If he does so, God's grace will help him improve his condition, softening the fierceness and tyranny of sin, bridling and mortifying the force of evil inclinations (Col 3:5) and giving strength to lead a virtuous life. By the grace of Christ Jesus we are made free from the law of sin and death (Rom 8:2), and so it is absolutely necessary for us to continue always in prayer and to add all manner of diligence and labor of our own.

Our Lord said, "Ask" and instructed us to pray, but when He added, "Seek," and "Knock," He thereby showed that we are to join our prayer with labor, diligence, and patience. This we must perseveringly continue to do not only in seeking spiritual blessings but also in seeking temporal ones.

It is the duty of every one of us to pray and labor not for himself alone but also for others, according to the injunction: "Pray for one another, that you may be healed" (James 5:16), and not merely one for another but also for our enemies, whom we are bound to love, however much our hearts may rebel from doing so. The Lord says, *Love your enemies*, and this love He describes by its effects: "Bless those who curse you, do good to those who hate you, and pray for those who spitefully use you and persecute you" (Matt 5:44). Therefore, it is our duty to pray for all mankind.

While we pray, we should also ask our brethren to assist us with similar prayers, following the example of the Apostle Paul (Eph 6:18; 1 Thess 3:1–3). More especially, we should ask the prayers of our spiritual fathers. We have an example of this even in the Old Testament Levitical books, where we repeatedly read that everyone who brought sin offerings was to appear by God's command before the priest, so that the priest would pray for him and seek God's pardon. In the New Testament we see the same in the Epistle of St James: "Is anyone among you sick? Let him call for the elders of the church, and let them pray over him ... And if he has committed sins, he will be forgiven" (James 5:14–15).

We should also desire and ask the same aid and help—that is, the prayers—of the saints, the servants and friends of God who now reign with Christ their Lord. This is a righteous and holy thing, for they too will join us in offering prayers to God for the forgiveness of sins. And when we repent, amend our lives, and receive pardon and mercy from the Lord, we may be sure that they too will rejoice over us, as well as the angels in heaven, as the Lord himself said (Luke 15:7, 10).

Here we must also speak of fasting, attentiveness, and sobriety, all of which the word of God joins with prayer: "But take heed to yourselves, lest your hearts be weighed down with carousing, drunkenness, and cares of this life" (Luke 21:34). "Be serious and watchful in your prayers" (1 Pet 4:7) "that ye may give yourselves to fasting and prayer" (1 Cor 7:5). Therefore, we also should in like manner offer our prayers, supplications, and thanksgivings with watchfulness and seriousness, and at the proper seasons also with fasting.

There are two forms of fasting—civil and religious. The first kind is otherwise called philosophical or natural; so far as prescribed by medical rules, it falls under the subject of diet. The second kind, the religious or ecclesiastical fast, is a holy and Christian observance. The difference between the two is this: the first depends solely on our own choice, and its object is to preserve health and enable us to perform our duties, but the ecclesiastical fast depends on Divine precept and so on faith and piety. The purpose of this kind is to humble ourselves before God, to subdue the force of carnal lusts, to assist us in true repentance, in prayer, in Divine Worship, and in other duties, and to obtain mercy and grace from God, as we are taught by many passages and examples in God's word.

Fasting is abstinence from all kind of food and drink or at the very least from all that is pleasant or superfluous. Such a fast as this was ordained by God Himself in the Old Testament to be observed at the yearly purification: "This shall be an ordinance forever for you: ... you shall humble your souls" with fasting (Lev 16:29–31). According to the example of this statute, whenever the Israelites repented before God, they always humbled their souls with fasting: "The sons of Israel were assembled with fasting, in sackcloth, and with dust on their heads ... and they stood in their place ... and confessing to the Lord and worshipping the Lord their God" (Neh 9:1, 3). (See also 1 Kings 7:6 LXX and Jer 6:9.)

Some holy fathers of the Church consider the beginning of fasting to be in paradise. St John Chrysostom, in his first sermon on Genesis, writes thus: "As gluttonous appetite is the source of countless evils for mankind, so also is fasting and the non-indulgence of the appetites of the belly the constant source to us of unspeakable benefits. Therefore God, when He had first made man and knew that this was the medicine he would most need for his soul's salvation, gave him, even at the very beginning of all, this first commandment, saying, 'Of every tree of the garden you may freely eat; but of the tree of the knowledge of good and evil you shall not eat.' By these words fasting was instituted." St Basil, in his first sermon on fasting, traces it to the same beginning.

Fasting was especially joined with prayer by all in the Old Testament at times when the Lord by His just judgment was preparing to bring any punishment on sinners. But even in this case, He Himself, solely in His love for mankind, willing to correct the children of Israel and to turn away His own just wrath, ordered all to fast and pray: "Blow the trumpet in Zion, consecrate a fast, call a sacred assembly, gather the people, sanctify the congregation" (Joel 2:15–16 (NKJV)). And such a public fast, joined with prayer, was always an effectual means of deliverance, as appears plainly from the same chapter, where the Lord, seeing them praying with fasting and weeping, turned His anger into mercy: "The Lord was zealous for His land and spared His people" (Joel 2:18–20).

In the New Testament, our Lord and Lawgiver Jesus Christ Himself fasted and in defending His disciples before the Pharisees He exempted them from fasting only while the Bridegroom was with them, but for all remaining time, after the Bridegroom would be taken away from them, He distinctly confirmed the duty (Matt 9:14–15; Luke 5:33–35). Furthermore, he instructed us how to fast, so that our fasting should not be like that of the Pharisees, nor have its reward from men, but from God (Matt 6:16–18). And again, the great Physician of our souls and bodies Himself showed how great is the power and benefit of fasting when, for the expulsion of a devil that had settled itself in a man, He prescribed no other medicine than prayer and fasting (Matt 17:21).

Here we may remark that fasting, as well as prayer itself, is said to be a service pleasing to God (Luke 2:37), for which reason the Apostles also, when they served the Lord, joined fasting with their prayers (Acts 13:2). Therefore, the ministers of the Lord's altar, and all who desire to serve or worship the Lord acceptably, in purity and sobriety, do only that which is becoming and their duty when they prepare themselves, according to the measure of their bodily strength, by fasting.

It is known to all that upon this foundation, that is, upon the words of God, Christ's Church of the New Testament has appointed yearly fasts and particular days of abstinence. This was done so that the children of the new Israel, through prayer to God, with fasting and contrition of heart and confession of their sins, would be brought to true repentance. Consequently, the fasts of the Church of the New Testament are nothing else than appointed times for repentance and days of yearly purification.

The Christians of the first ages observed moderation and temperance always, and at fit seasons fasting also, joined with prayer, as the special marks among themselves of an honorable Christian life and decent civil society, and at all times they abhorred luxury and excess. To this St Clement of Alexandria bears testimony in the first and second books of *The Instructor.*

However, it is absolutely necessary that he who keeps outward fasts also fasts spiritually, that is, he who fasts and prays outwardly must at the same time avoid all sin and unrighteousness and be charitable and diligent in every good work. For "prayer is good with fasting, almsgiving, and righteousness" (Tob 12:8). But if any man keeps the fasts extremely strictly, but remains without charity or honesty to his neighbor, such a fast is not acceptable to God:

"If you fast for condemnations and quarrels, and to strike a humble man with your fists, why do you fast to Me as you do today, so your voice may be heard in crying? I did not choose this fast, and such a day for a man to humble his soul; nor if you should bow your neck like a ring and spread sackcloth and ashes under yourself, could you thus call such a fast acceptable. I did not choose such a fast." Says the Lord: "rather loose every bond of wrongdoing; untie the knots of violent dealings; cancel the debts of the oppressed; and tear apart every unjust contract. Break your bread for the hungry, and bring the homeless poor into your house. If you see a naked man, clothe him, nor shall you disregard your offspring in your own household. Then your light shall break forth as the morning, and your healing shall spring forth quickly. Your righteousness shall go before you, and the glory of God shall cover you. Then you shall call cry out and God will hear you. While you are still speaking He will say, 'Behold I am here'" (Isa 58:4–9).

Similar instruction is also given by the Lord through the Prophet Zechariah (see chapters 7 and 8 of the Book of Zechariah). See also St John Chrysostom, in his fourth sermon on Genesis, for a very profitable discussion on the same subject.

Where fasting and sobriety are not practiced, but instead of them continual overeating and drunkenness, countless mischiefs will be engendered, spiritual, no less than bodily (James 4:1). In such people that sanctification and honor in which the apostle admonishes every one to possess his vessel will find no place (1 Thess 4:4–7), but they will become the dwelling-places only of fierce, brutal, and devilish passions (Matt 12:44–45), as is shown beyond any doubt by the dissoluteness and overthrow of Sodom and other examples.

St John Chrysostom, in his first homily on Genesis, writes thus: "See how Divine Scripture always reproves a life of indulgence! At one time it says, 'The people sat down to eat and drink, and rose up to play,' at another, 'Jeshurun ate and drank, grew fat, thick, and broad, and apostatized.' And the people of Sodom, beside their other sins, by this sin most of all drew down upon themselves God's wrath and destruction from heaven, for hear what the prophet said, 'This was the iniquity of Sodom,' for it was in fullness of bread and wine that they fell to lust after evil pleasures, and so intemperance is, as it were, the source and root of all evils."

In order to be able to observe the order of prayer and all other duties connected with it, we have the greatest need of spiritual sobriety and vigilance, nor can we neglect these duties as regards the body. This rule is prescribed us by our Lord Jesus Christ Himself: "Take heed, watch, and pray; … And what I say to you, I say to all: Watch!" (Mark 13:33,37) (Matt 24:42). "Behold, I am coming as a thief. Blessed is he who watches, and keeps his garments, lest he walk naked and they see his shame" (Rev 16:15). And the Apostles also, in the spirit of Christ's words, exhort us to do the same: "Be sober, be vigilant" (1 Pet 5:8.); "Let us not sleep, as do others, but let us watch and be sober" (1 Thess 5:6). Such attentiveness and sobriety are no less necessary for

Christians than eyes are for our bodies or the light of the sun for our eyes.

Sobriety is necessary for one's entire life because without it a person cannot keep himself in order. Sobriety is not merely to not be "weighed down with carousing, and drunkenness, and cares of this life" (Luke 21:34) but also in keeping ourselves free from the inward passions of anger, envy, covetousness, and the like. For all these passions darken the inner eye of the heart and deprive us of sound reason, no less than drunkenness. Therefore, the Apostles Peter and James exhort us to "lay aside all malice, all deceit, hypocrisy, envy, and all evil speaking," … and "gird up the loins of your mind, be sober, and rest your hope fully upon the grace that is to be brought to you at the revelation of Jesus Christ" (1 Peter 2:1; 1:13). (See also James 1:21).

All these things—fasting, attentiveness, sobriety, prayers night and day, ascetic labors and struggles—are appointed in the Lord's commandments solely to help us become holy and blameless before God in the faith of the Gospel and in love, that is, to fill us with the fruits of the Holy Spirit. But if these are not found in us, then all our prayers and labors will profit us nothing, as the example of the five foolish virgins plainly shows (Matt 25:10–13).

St Macarius, in his first sermon *On Keeping the Heart*, writes thus:

If we will not be adorned with humility, simplicity, and goodness, the outward form of prayer profits us nothing, and this we say not of prayer only, but also of every kind of struggle and ascetic labor: virginity, attentiveness, or any other labor that may be performed for the sake of virtue. If, I say, we do not bear the fruits of love, peace, joy, meekness, humility, sincerity, simplicity, faith, and patience abundant in ourselves, all our work and struggle will be vain and unprofitable. For every work and every struggle ought to be undertaken for the sake of these fruits, and if the fruits of love and peace are not found in us, all we do remains vain and without effect. For they who labor without having these will appear as those five foolish virgins at the Day of Judgment. Those virgins, since they did not take

146 A PRACTICAL HANDBOOK FOR PRIESTLY MINISTRY

spiritual oil—which means the above-mentioned virtues—in the vessels of their hearts, are therefore called foolish and are refused entrance to the spiritual wedding of the King. All the trouble they had taken to preserve their virginity, through the lack of spiritual virtue and the absence in them of the manifest in-dwelling of the Holy Spirit, is made of no account.

Motives and incitements to pray and struggle in all the above-mentioned duties include the following:

1. The commandments that God has given us to pray, mentioned in preceding sections.
2. The exceeding mercy of God to those who pray, as it is written, "For Thou, Lord, art good and gentle, and of great mercy unto all them that call upon Thee" (Ps 85:5 LXX), "to all such as call upon [Thee] in truth" (Ps 144:18 LXX).
3. God's most sweet and unfailing promises to hear our prayers and to grant us forgiveness: "for He who promised is faithful" (Heb 10:23).
4. Our Lord Jesus Christ is the Son of God and God everlasting before all worlds (John 1:1), but as man He is "one Mediator between God and men" … "who gave Himself a ransom for all" (1 Tim 2:5–6). He "also makes intercession for us" (Rom 8:34). Therefore, though we ourselves are unworthy to approach our Heavenly Father or ask Him for good things, yet through the intercession of so great a Mediator, even Jesus Christ Himself, we have access to the Father (Eph 2:18) and He accepts our petitions.
5. "The Holy Spirit Himself bears witness with our spirit … helps us in our weaknesses" and "makes intercession for us with groanings which cannot be uttered" (Rom 8:16,26).
6. Even our common name of Christian must impel us to offer up in our thoughts to God spiritual sacrifices of prayers and thanksgiving (1 Pet 2:5–7; Rom 12:1–2).
7. Owing to the necessities and infirmities both of our souls and bodies, we all need God's help, and, because of our many sins, we require forgiveness and mercy.

8. The greatest punishments and miseries await those who neglect to pray in contempt of the Lord's commandments and with carelessness about the future. All these reasons we have mentioned have great weight and whoever will weigh them attentively will doubtless be roused from the sleep of sloth and give himself diligently to prayer.

No less strong are those motives and incitements to prayer that are found in the fruits of prayer:

1. Prayer makes the Holy Spirit dwell in the hearts of men (Luke 11:13).
2. Through prayer true faith develops in person's soul and increases.
3. Through prayer we receive from the Lord's own hand all spiritual and temporal gifts.
4. Through prayer we overcome sin, dispel afflictions, feel comfort in our hearts, and are armed against various temptations, even against the devil himself.
5. Through prayer we obtain everlasting salvation, as it is written, "Whoever calls on the name of the Lord shall be saved" (Acts 2:21). And he who gives himself to prayer shows that he does not scorn God's promises, but is convinced that they are all to be highly valued, that the Lord our God is true, "and that there is no unrighteousness in Him" (Ps 91:16 LXX).

On the other hand, how many and how great are the evils that ensue wherever prayer is neglected, especially if the neglect proceeds from contempt and pride.

1. Such people break God's commandment.
2. Such people scorn the inestimable promises of God, instead of appreciating them, whereby they despise His mercy.
3. In such people the Holy Spirit can find no place to rest.
4. In such people faith gradually dwindles and goes out at last, for prayer is the food of faith and of all other virtues.
5. Such people are bold to do every shameful thing, and they rapidly and easily descend from one sin to another. As a result, they become exposed with no defense to many temptations, dangers, and calamities.

6. Such people deprive themselves of all God's spiritual gifts, and so finally also of His kingdom, since all these things are given by God's mercy only through prayer. Therefore, whoever neglects to pray out of contempt or carelessness has not yet really come to know his Lord, nor has he considered the Lord's commandments as he ought to consider them. Concerning such people we may well say, as God said of His people, "The ox knows its owner, and the donkey its master's crib; but Israel does not know Me, and the people do not understand Me" (Isa 1:3).

It will be profitable here to mention briefly that our prayers and those things that help our prayers, such as fasting, attentiveness, and sobriety, are most efficacious when they are offered in the following ways:

1. With faith, in spirit, and in truth: "whatever things you ask in prayer, believing, you will receive" (Matt 21: 22).
2. In the name of Jesus Christ: "Most assuredly, I say to you, whatever you ask the Father in My name He will give you" (John 16:23). The same is confirmed in many other places.
3. In the fear of God: "He will fulfill the desire of them that fear Him, and He will hear their prayer, and save them" (Ps 144:19 LXX).
4. With humility and contrition of heart: "The sacrifice unto God is a contrite spirit; a contrite and humble heart God shall not despise" (Ps 50:17 LXX).
5. With the spirit of forgiveness and reconciliation toward our neighbors, as regards their offences against us: "Whenever you stand praying, if you have anything against anyone, forgive him, that your Father in heaven may also forgive you your trespasses" (Mark 11:25).
6. Without wrath or doubt: "I desire therefore that men pray everywhere, lifting up holy hands, without wrath and doubting" (1 Tim. 2:8).
7. If our petitions are agreeable to the will of God: "If we ask anything according to His will, He hears us" (1 John 5:14).

It often happens that good ceases to be good when it is done for the wrong reasons, and so even prayer can become displeasing to God, and virtues can become fruitless to him that prays in the following circumstances:

1. When prayer is offered hypocritically: "And when you pray, you shall not be like the hypocrites" (Matt 6:5).
2. When prayer is offered without faith: "He who doubts is like a wave of the sea driven and tossed by the wind. For let not that man suppose that he will receive anything from the Lord" (James 1:6–7).
3. When a man prays for anything with an evil intention: "You ask and do not receive, because you ask amiss, that you may spend it on your pleasures" (James 4:3).
4. When he who prays is proud and judges his neighbor: "I am not like other men ... or even as this tax collector" (Luke 18:11).
5. When we do not forgive our neighbors their trespasses: "If you do not forgive men their trespasses, neither will your Father forgive your trespasses" (Matt 6:15).

Furthermore, we must take special notice of two causes that will prevent God from hearing our prayers:

1. When we turn away our ears from God's words and will not listen to them, then the Lord also will turn away from us. Of this He Himself speaks in the Proverbs with anger: "Since I called, ... but you paid no attention. But made My counsels invalid, ... Consequently, I will laugh at your annihilation, ... And when destructions comes to you. For it shall be, when you call upon me, I will not listen to you" (Prov 1:25–30 LXX). The same is confirmed in Isaiah 65:12 and in Jeremiah 7:13 and in 11:7–8.
2. Even if a person does hear the word of God or reads it himself, the Lord will not accept his prayers if he does not live according to God's law, at least until he repents. God Himself speaks of this through the Prophet Isaiah: "When you stretch forth your hands to Me, I will turn My eyes from you. Although you make many prayers, I will not listen to you. Your hands are full

of blood" (Isa 1:15). "Although you should bring fine wheat flour, it is vain. Incense is an abomination to Me. I cannot endure your new moons, and Sabbaths, and the calling of assemblies and fasting and holy day" (Isa 1:13). And afterwards He shows them the means, that is, repentance, through which He will mercifully listen to the prayer of those who entreat Him: "Wash yourselves, make yourselves clean. Put away the evils from your souls before My eyes" (Isa 1:16). "Although your sins are like crimson, I shall make them white like snow" (Isa 1:18). Therefore, prayer must be accompanied with true repentance.

It must now be clear that prayer to the Lord, whether public or private, is an essential part of that service that we owe to God, and it is of such nature in itself that whenever we duly perform it, we by the very act itself confess our true God to be indeed God almighty, all-present, all-wise, and all-good (this truth is grounded on the first four of the Lord's commandments). By this confession, we reveal by our actions that He is our God, that "it is He that hath made us, and not we ourselves, for we are His people, and the sheep of His pasture" (Ps 99:3 LXX).

Not only do we come to this acknowledgment of our Creator by means of prayer but by speaking to Him as children to their Father and entreating His love, we receive from Him the power of the Holy Spirit, Who enlightens our mind, moves our heart, and teaches us always to cry to Him: "Abba, Father!" And so drawing near to Him, we are made to be, as the apostle writes, "no longer strangers and foreigners, but fellow citizens with the saints and members of the household of God," that is, God's own people (Eph 2:19).

Let no one then despise or neglect prayer, which is the greatest means appointed by God for our salvation. For all, from the least even to the greatest, are bound to call out with a pure heart to the Lord God almighty and to offer to Him, and to Him alone, as is His due, all honor, glory, praise, thanksgiving, and worship, according to the commandment, "You shall worship the Lord your God, and Him only you shall serve" (Matt 4:10).

CHAPTER 14

☒☒☒

Prayer as the Special Duty of Priests

When Lord Himself ordained the order of the services of the Old Testament Church, He appointed for it certain special persons, namely Aaron and the Levites, giving them the commandment to pray: "So this shall be an ordinance forever for you, to make atonement for the children of Israel, for all their sins" (Lev 16:34). "So the priest shall make atonement for the whole congregation of the children of Israel, and it shall be [forgiven] them" (Num 15:25).

Although the Lord has commanded all to pray without exception, in the New Testament His commandment applies with double force to the order of the priesthood, since priests are appointed for His service (Heb 5:2–4). More especially is this true in those cases where He addressed the commandment directly to the Apostles: "Ask, and you will receive, that your joy may be full" (John 16:24). And a little before He had given the means: "Most assuredly, I say to you, whatever you ask the Father in My Name He will give you" (John 16:23). Similarly, before He suffered, He especially exhorted His disciples to pray: "Why do you sleep? Rise and pray, lest you enter into temptation" (Luke 22:46).

The Apostles, following the example of their Lord, whenever they mentioned the duty of teaching that was laid upon them, spoke at the same time of prayer as a duty inseparable from the other: "But we will give ourselves continually to prayer and to the ministry of the word" (Acts 6:4). The Apostle Paul, in his instructions to Timothy, Bishop of Ephesus, exhorts and entreats all priests to pray before all things: "I exhort first of all that supplications, prayers, intercessions, and giving of thanks be made for all men, for kings and all who are in authority" (1 Tim 2:1–2). The Apostle James likewise mentions this as the duty of the priesthood: "Is anyone among you sick? Let him call for the elders of the church, and let them pray over him" (James 5:14). Thus, both the Lord and His apostles clearly taught us that the duty of prayer is in a special manner laid upon the priestly order, and it is inseparably conjoined with their other duty of teaching.

St John Chrysostom, in his sixth homily on Timothy, has these words: "The priest is as it were a common father of the whole universe, for it is his duty to take thought for all. For this reason the Apostle Paul says, 'I exhort first of all that prayers … be made.'"

The same commandments and Christ's own example show the priests what and for whom they should pray and ask for God's goodness. He, after His Last and mystical Supper, being our great Highpriest of good things to come "who has passed through the heaven" (Heb 4:14), as man prayed for us, for the apostles, and for all who would believe in Him to the Father concerning the preaching of the Gospel: Father "I have given to them the words which You have given Me; and they have received them, and have known surely that I came from You … Sanctify them by Your truth. Your word is truth … And for their sakes I sanctify Myself, that they also may be sanctified by the truth." "I do not pray for these alone, but also for those who will believe in Me through their word." "Holy Father, keep through Your Name those whom You have given Me." "Keep them from the evil one" (John 17:8, 17, 19, 20, 11, 15). And besides this example of His own most holy prayer, He gave an express commandment to pray for the preaching of the Gospel: "Therefore pray to the Lord of the harvest to send out laborers into His harvest" (Matt 9:38).

The Apostles did in fact pray most earnestly for the preaching of the Gospel: Lord "grant to Your servants that with all boldness they may speak Your word" (Acts 4:29). The Apostle Paul not only prayed himself but asked others also for their prayers that the Lord would give him power and strength to preach the Gospel (Col 4:3). And, like Christ, they also prayed for all believers (Acts 14:22–24). We read that Paul, together with all the priests of the Church of Ephesus, kneeled down and prayed for the faithful (Acts 20:36). All the Apostolic Epistles attest to this, especially Paul's. For to whatever people he preached, and to whomever he wrote, he always prayed for them with incomparable zeal that they might know the true God, that holy faith might develop and be perfected in them, that Christian love and all other virtues might be increased (Rom 1:9–10; Eph 1:16–17).

St Basil the Great in his Canons drawn from the New Testament, in Part LXX, chapter 14, has these words: "The pastor and teacher of the Gospel should pray for the people, so that by his preaching they may progress in faith and holy life, and for all his success he should give thanks to the Lord. Therefore, it is the duty of every priest to pray for his parishioners, that their faith should not fail (Luke 22:32)".

It is our duty to pray to the Most High also for all the authorities of government that they may be guided by God's Spirit to act in the performance of their duties, and in their whole lives, as He requires of them: "That we may lead a quiet and peaceable life in all godliness and reverence. For this is good and acceptable in the sight of God our Saviour" (1 Tim 2:2–3).

The Lord in His word requires the following of all authorities and rulers set by God over the people:

1. As regards themselves, they should be religious men, "such as fear God, just men, hating covetousness" (Exod 18:21). They should be wise and understanding (Deut 1:13).
2. As regards all who are under them, they should be zealous for the common good and constantly endeavor to preserve quiet and good order among the people, but at the same time they should punish evil men with discretion and protect the innocent, so that crimes and vices of all kinds may decrease, and virtue may everywhere flourish (Rom 13:3–4; 1 Pet 2:14).
3. As regards all cases which may come before them, they must be impartial and just: "Hear the cases between your brethren, and judge righteously between a man and his brother or the resident alien with him. You shall not show partiality in judgment; you shall judge the small and the great; you shall not shrink before any

man's presence, for the judgment is God's" (Deut 1:16–17). Further, the Lord, among other things, forbids receiving bribes: "they shall not pervert judgment … nor take a bribe, for a bribe blinds the eyes of the wise and twists the words of the righteous" (Deut 16:19).

The Lord commanded priests to pray for all the sins of the children of Israel, for we all sin much and continually (James 3:2) and many nets and snares surrounding us everywhere lure us to sin. This we cannot fail to see from nearly every day's experience in life. Therefore, in order for us and our people to obtain from God the merciful forgiveness of our sins and to be ever defended from all snares of the enemy—whether open or secret—it is absolutely necessary for priests, as shepherds chosen for this very thing, to unceasingly implore the Divine Goodness.

But in order for "the body of sin [to] be done away with, we should no longer be slaves of sin" (Rom 6:6), and in order for no sins—especially those that lead to death (1 John 5:16) or those that cause us to cry out to heaven (Gen 18:20–21)—to have dominion over us (Rom 6:12–14) we all need to be led by God's Spirit "not as slaves to uncleanness, and of lawlessness leading to more lawlessness" but "as slaves of righteousness to holiness" (Rom 6:19). The pastors of the Church, besides the word of diligent instruction to the people, must also labor with most fervent prayers to God, especially when they stand before His altar, entreating Him to pour out the power of the Holy Spirit and to put His fear in the hearts of His people, for the extinction of all impure and ungodly living, which is the source of all miseries and evils to the whole world (Jer 4:17–18).

The prayers of St Basil the Great appointed for the Sixth and Ninth Hours are to this purpose, and there are other prayers in reference to various necessities in the other Hours and the Inter-hours. Also, some of the priest's prayers for Vespers and Matins in the service book are useful, and priests can also use them devoutly at home, no less than in church, to entreat God's goodness and to give thanks. Also, many of David's Psalms are proper for different occasions and necessities, and a careful priest who thinks of his salvation and his people's will not fail to use them. But in all cases let the Lord's Prayer be said first.

From evils that spring from within come those that are outward also, as from bitter seeds grow even bitterer fruits. Often people are obliged to endure various calamities and misfortunes because of their sins, but in all these, they have no other refuge but God: "God is our refuge and strength, a very present helper in the troubles which greatly afflict us" (Ps 45:1 LXX). He has Himself given us a commandment, saying: "And call upon Me in the day of thy trouble, and I will deliver thee" (Ps 49:15 LXX). And so priests, as public guides and intercessors, should in temporal calamities also lead everyone by example, both the community at large and families and individuals in private life, with fervent prayers to God.

With regard to the community at large, it is the duty of priests in time of continued bad weather to pray for such a change as may suit the needs of those living off the land. In time of drought, he should pray for showers, so that the earth may bring forth her fruit: "Ask for yourself rain from the Lord" (Zech 10:1), and in time of war they should pray for victory over the enemy, following the examples of Moses against Amalek (Exod 17), Gideon against Midian (Judg 7–8), and the like.

With regard to private individuals, the priest should pray for the comfort of the afflicted, for the delivery and freedom of the captive, and for the recovery and health of the sick, together with the forgiveness of their sins (James 5:15), for the gift of patience to the persecuted, for speedy help, support, and defense for those in the agony of death, and the like, as the case may be.

But when the Lord, because of the multiplication of sin and unrighteousness, and because of man's contempt for His judgments, either threatens to punish or actually punishes any city or country with famine, pestilence, earthquake, or any other grievous plague, in such cases the duty of the priests is to do the following:

1. To exhort all the people in common to repentance, so that all of them will cease their evil ways and turn back to the Lord, as it is

written: Repent, "and turn away from all your ungodliness, and it shall not be to you as a punishment" (Ezek 18:30). "Turn to Me with all your heart, with fasting and wailing and with mourning; rend your heart, and not your garments ... for [the Lord] is merciful and compassionate" (Joel 2:12–13).

2. Priests should, with the deepest devotion, set themselves as a wall between God and the people, following the example of Moses and other prophets, and with contrition of heart fall down before Him and pray, and so turn away God's just wrath: "Between the porch and the altar, the priests of the altar ministering to the Lord, will each be weeping and will say, 'O Lord, spare Your people'" (Joel 2:17).

Such a wall was Moses (Exod 32:11). "Moses prayed to the Lord; and the fire was quenched" (Num 11:2). Of which David also makes mention: "And He said He would have destroyed them, had not Moses His chosen stood before Him in the breach, to turn away His wrathful indignation, lest He should destroy them" (Ps 105:23 LXX). So Aaron "stood between the dead and the living; so the plague ceased" (Num 17:13 LXX). Other prophets did likewise, such as Samuel (1 Kg 6 LXX), Isaiah (chapters 63 and 64), Daniel (chapter 9), Jeremiah (14:7), 1 Esdras (chapter 9 LXX), Nehemiah (chapter 9), and others. "These called upon the Lord" confessing in their own persons the sins of the whole people, "and He heard them ... for they kept His testimonies" (Ps 98:6–7).

Here it will be fitting and profitable to note that when the Lord brings any public chastisement upon a people, He, as it were, looks down from heaven to see if there is anyone who can stand before the Lord, stay His wrath, and turn it to mercy: "'So I sought for a man among them who would conduct himself rightly and stand before Me perfectly at all times in the land, so as not to wipe her out completely; but I did not find him. Therefore I poured out My anger in the fire of my wrath to finish them, and I recompensed their ways on their own heads,' says the Lord" (Ezek 22:30–31). And, in consideration of this, pastors ought to give heed to themselves and the signs of God's judgment. For if any man, then certainly a priest is much more bound to be living righteously, and stand earnestly before the Lord, especially in time of national calamity, so that the word of the Lord above mentioned will not be spoken of them nor the words that He spoke through the Prophet Jeremiah, saying, "For the shepherds act foolishly and no longer seek out the Lord" (Jer 10:17 LXX).

We have said above that it is the priest's duty in every kind or branch of teaching to instill into the hearts of his listeners the knowledge of Jesus Christ the Son of God and faith in Him. Listen, then, priests! This is what we should also make the very first object of our prayers, and with the apostle we should bow our knees to our Heavenly Father and beseech Him without ceasing to fill all the faithful with His heavenly knowledge and grant "that Christ may dwell in [their] hearts through faith" (Eph 3:17). Then we may begin "to know the love of Christ, which passes knowledge" (Eph 3:19). And if we will indeed become filled with these supernatural gifts from our Saviour, then, in all adversities, whatever we ask in Christ's Name, we will receive. What is more, everything that occurs will inevitably be for our own benefit. "He who did not spare His own Son, but delivered Him up for us all, how shall He not with Him also freely give us all things?" (Rom 8:32).

The apostle has ordered that with prayers and supplications *thanks* also should be given to the Lord for all men (1 Tim 2:1). Even nature itself suggests the same. If anyone does something good to us, we love and honor him and give him thanks, and who is there that so fills us with benefits as God? (Ps 144:9 LXX) "In Him we live and move and have our being" (Acts 17:28). From His hand we receive all things needful and profitable, both for the temporal life and for the life to come (Ps 103:28 LXX). Therefore, it necessarily follows that we should give thanks to the Lord for all things with love and devotion, lest it be said of us as of others in olden times: "And they forgat His good deeds, and the wonderful works that He had showed for them" (Ps 77:11 LXX) and there were "not any found who returned to give glory to God" (Luke 17:18).

When the apostle said, "In every thing give thanks; for this is the will of God in Jesus Christ for you" (1 Thess 5:18), he gave us to understand that it is our duty to thank God not only when in prosperity and enjoying God's bounties but also when suffering affliction or any special discipline from the hand of the Most High. Even if death itself is near, even then we must join with prayer "giving thanks always for all things to God the Father in the name of our Lord Jesus Christ" (Eph 5:20), following the example of the Apostles (Acts 5:41; 16:25).

St John Chrysostom, in his nineteenth homily on Ephesians, writes thus:

> Let your petitions be made known together with thanksgiving to God, for nothing is so pleasing to God as to see a man thankful. We must especially thank Him when we have been able to withdraw our soul from the vices of lying, wrath, bitterness, dishonesty, impurity, fornication, and covetousness; and to purify it with the virtues contrary to such vices. What then? Ought we to give thanks for everything that befalls us? Certainly we must, even if it is sickness, even if it is poverty. For if in the Old Testament a certain wise man taught, saying, "Whatsoever may be brought upon you, receive it all with love, and in the changes of thy humiliation be patient," much more should this be so in the New. Even if you lack for words, still say, "I thank Thee!" for that is thanksgiving. But if—when you receive benefits and abound in all things, and are happy and prosperous—you give thanks, this is nothing great or wonderful. What is sought of you is to give thanks in afflictions, in sicknesses, in difficulties, in distresses. Utter nothing before these words, "I thank Thee, O Lord!" And why do I speak of afflictions here? We ought to thank God even for hell itself, its pains and torments. For it greatly profits us—if we attend to it—to have the fear of hell put as a bridle on our heart ... When we are in poverty, when we are in sickness, when we are in danger, let us then enlarge our thanksgiving; thanksgiving, I mean, not by words or the tongue, but let us thank Him in act and deed, with our minds, our hearts, and our souls: for He loves us more than they who begat us.

The injunctions and examples set down here refer to prayers and supplications for the living, but the priest, as the steward of the Mysteries of God, must also pray for the departed, in the hope and faith of the resurrection of those who have fallen asleep. Of this we have certain assurance both from the Scriptures and from Christ's Holy Church in Apostolic and early times.

The Prophet Baruch, among other things, prays for the dead: "O Lord Almighty, the God of Israel, hear the prayer of the dead of Israel … Do not remember the wrongdoings of our fathers" (Bar 3:4–5). In the second book of Maccabees it is written: "Thus they all blessed the ways of the Lord, the righteous judge, who reveals the hidden things. They turned to supplication and prayed that the sin they had committed might be completely blotted out … [The noble Judas] then took up an offering from his soldiers amounting to two thousand silver drachmas, and sent it to Jerusalem to present as a sin offering. In doing so he acted properly and with honor, taking note of the resurrection … Thus he made atonement for the fallen, so as to set them free from their transgression" (2 Macc 12:41–46).

The successors of the Apostles in the first centuries and the Fathers of the Church give us the strongest testimonies on this point, but it will be enough to select one or two places. The holy martyr Cyprian in certain of his Epistles distinctly mentions the commemoration of the departed in the Bloodless Sacrifice. St Basil the Great, in his Liturgy, and in his prayers for the Day of Pentecost, made prayers for the dead. St John Chrysostom, in his third moral on Philippians, among other things, writes as follows: "It was not for nothing that this was ordained by the Apostles, that at the dread Mysteries commemorations should be made for the departed." In his twenty-first moral on Acts, he writes: "Not in vain are the oblations that we offer for the departed; not in vain are the prayers; not in vain are the alms. All these things have been prescribed by the Holy Spirit." See also the same Father's forty-first moral on 1 Corinthians in his sixth book *On the Priesthood* (ch. 4).

All the above-mentioned forms of prayer and thanksgiving are profitable and agreeable to the will of God. Therefore, the pastors of the Church are bound to the constant discharge of this duty not only on Sundays and feast days in the churches with the congregation but also in their own homes and in all other places, alone, as circumstances allow.

St John Chrysostom, in his fourth moral on 2 Thessalonians, writes thus: "Not in the church only, but also at home, before everything else I make prayers for your health spiritual and temporal. For there is no other prayer that so befits a priest, as that which he makes for the welfare of his people, before he approaches God to pray for his own. For if Job, when he arose, prayed immediately for his children only after the flesh, how much more ought we for our spiritual children to do the same?" And the same Father, in his second homily on Romans, has these words: "Can anyone boast that when he prays at home he remembers the entire congregation of his church? I think not. But Paul approached God not for one city only, but in a manner for the entire world, and this not once, not twice, not thrice, but without ceasing." Also, in his fifteenth moral on 2 Corinthians, Samuel showed himself great when he said, "Far be it from me to sin against the Lord in ceasing to pray for you" (1 Kgs 12:23).

Nor is it less true that the ministry of the Divine Mysteries requires in itself fervent prayer from the priest that he may not in ministering, or after having ministered, sin in the Lord's sight, nor fall under the severity of God's judgment, like Nadab and Abihu (Leviticus Chapter 10) and others. Therefore, every priest, to be able to perform at all times the service of the Church without blame, must earnestly entreat the Lord to bestow upon him the power of the Holy Spirit. For He alone, as the One Who first appoints and makes men priests through the laying on of the bishop's hands, afterwards in the work of their ministry, makes them able ministers of the New Testament, who do not need to be ashamed (2 Cor 3:6).

More especially is this required of the priest during the Service of the Divine Liturgy, for this is not only the Mystery that Christ instituted at His Last and Mystical Supper (Matt 26:26; Luke 22:14; John 6:51) but this is the commemoration of the entire economy of our salvation, wrought by our Lord Jesus Christ the Son of God, according to the commandment: "Do this in remembrance of Me" (1 Cor 11:24). Hence, everyone must see of what surpassing greatness is this service of the priest.

St John Chrysostom, in his third book *On the Priesthood* (ch. 4), writes thus:

> Do you wish to see the excellence of this priestly service? Picture to yourself Elijah with all the multitude of the people standing around him; the sacrifice is lying on the stones; and all the rest standing in silence and breathless attention, while the Prophet alone is praying. Suddenly, the fire falls from heaven upon the sacrifice. Here is a miracle, and one most striking and terrifying. But pass from that to what is being done now. Here you will see not only miracles, but miracles beyond all wonder, overpowering. The priest stands bringing down not fire, but the Holy Spirit. He prays for a long time, not that a material flame may fall from above to devour what lies before him, but that Grace, coming down on the Sacrifice, may inflame the souls of all and make them brighter than any silver purified in the fire. Who then can think lightly of this most tremendous Mystery? Who, but he that is either an idiot, or a madman?

The greater and more excellent this Mystery, the greater the danger and the greater the need for caution in its service. Here the minister of the Lord's altar must give most diligent heed to himself, practicing extraordinary purity and sobriety and showing extraordinary devotion, lest his ministry turn to his own condemnation. Therefore, he must prepare himself for it beforehand in both soul and body, according to the commandments given in Scripture: "Let the priests who come near the Lord God sanctify themselves, lest He destroy some of them" (Exod 19:22). "When they go into the tabernacle of testimony, they shall wash with water; lest they die" (Exod 30:20). That is, let them purify themselves from all filthiness of the flesh and spirit, and so, having duly prepared themselves, let them stand before the face of God and perfect Holiness in His fear (2 Cor 7:1–2).

St John Chrysostom, in his sixth book *On the Priesthood*, writes thus:

> When the priest stands before the altar to invoke the Holy Spirit and to consummate the most tremendous sacrifice and to touch repeatedly with his hands the one Lord of all, at that moment, tell me, what purity, what devotion must not be required of him! Think, what hands should they be, which are used for this service! What tongue, which is to utter such words! Who shall be so pure and holy as to receive into his soul so great a Spirit? At that time angels stand with the priest, and the whole order of the heavenly powers cry aloud, and fill the space round about the altar, in adoration of Him Who lies there.

The very nature and essence of this Mystery, as well as its miraculous effects, sweetly invite our hearts to this preparation: "He who eats My Flesh and drinks My Blood abides in Me, and I in Him … He who eats this Bread will live for ever" (John 6:56, 58). However, fear and terror inspire in us the thought of the consequences if we are unprepared or lacking in devoutness: "Therefore whoever eats this bread or drinks this cup of the Lord in an unworthy manner will be guilty of the body and blood of the Lord." Such a minister eats and drinks "judgment to himself" (1 Cor 11:27, 29). And if all who approach unworthily incur so fearful a judgment, then certainly the priest who ministers this Sacrament unworthily will incur a double judgment, a double portion of torment. Firstly, since he ministers unworthily; secondly, since he eats and drinks unworthily, not considering the Body and Blood of the Lord.

Therefore, the consumption of the Holy Gifts in the altar demands great attention and reverence. Haste and disruption of order are impermissible here. A bow, a kiss to the holy altar table, and careful taking of the Holy Body with the left hand. The placing of it upon the right hand. If there is a bishop, a kiss to his shoulder and a calm movement back to the altar table, under no circumstances behind the backs of the other clergy. The reading of the prayer; a reverent blessing of oneself with the Holy Body and communion. All should be done with profound faith and fear, in silence, without commotion and careless chewing.

Conversation, brazenness, and rapidity on the part of him who is consuming make a bad impression on the faithful and truly are not in keeping with the sublimity of the Holy Mysteries. I have seen a deacon not even cross himself before and after consuming the Holy Gifts. It is bad for the person consuming to suck on or to lick out the spoon and chalice. When communing of the Holy Blood one must not, under any circumstances, insert the napkin into the collar of the cassock onto one's sweaty neck. The communion of the faithful needs to be also carried out with great care, attention, patience, and love.

Give heed to yourself, priest. Remember that Moses, when he went up to the Mount that smoked with fire, said of himself: "I am exceedingly afraid and trembling" but you draw near not to the Mount that may be touched, but to "Mount Zion and to the city of the living God … to God the Judge of all, … to Jesus the Mediator of the new covenant, and to the blood of sprinkling that speaks better things than that of Abel" (Heb 12:22–24). Consequently, you should approach and stand with fear and devotion, much more than Moses himself. It was said to Moses at the bush: "*Take your sandals off your feet.*" You must also take off the sandals of carnal lust from the feet of your soul, "*for the place where you stand is holy ground.*" He was devout when looking up at the Lord God, you must be the same, for you have to stand before the very face of God. Isaiah saw the Lord and was humbled (Isa 20). Ezekiel saw the glory of the Lord and fell on his face (Ezek 1:28). Daniel also was vouchsafed a vision of the Lord, and he fell down and lay on the ground and trembled in fear and terror (Dan 10:9). But to you the Lord has vouchsafed the grace of His priesthood and has called you to minister at the altar of His glory. You must, therefore, also fear and fall down both with your soul and with your body, praying with humility and devotion. This is the purpose and intent of the examples given above—to prepare yourself before ministering. Indeed, the very substance of the prayers of the Divine Liturgy of St Basil the Great and St John Chrysostom suffices to assure you of this truth. Your duty is to be attentive.

Before concluding this chapter, we must remind priests that it is not enough if they are themselves zealous and practiced in prayer, but they are further absolutely bound by their calling to teach others how to pray, as Christ taught His Apostles, and they taught theirs (Luke 11:1).

For the beginner those prayers that are printed in the prayer books and catechisms will suffice. In order to help them learn the prayers by heart—and always utter them in spirit and in truth, as in the presence of God—it is the duty of priests to take all possible diligence in teaching beginners and never to cease until they have learned perfectly.

When teaching people how to pray, priests should earnestly exhort both parents and their children to read the appointed evening and morning prayers, to begin all their labors with prayer, and to end them with thanksgiving, so that the Lord will bless all their labors and work. It would be especially laudable and profitable if parish priests, as well as lesser clergy, would teach the children of their parish, from six or seven to nine or ten years old, to learn the prayers and God's commandments by heart. For between those ages children mostly spend their time in doing nothing, though they are capable of learning a great deal.

The commandment of the Lord requires that besides praying at home, Christians must also pray together in the church: "Enter into His gates with thanksgiving, and into His courts with praise; be thankful unto Him, and praise His Name" (Ps 99:4 LXX). Therefore, it is the priest's duty to explain that all are bound not only to pray at home but also to come to the House of the Lord on Sundays and feast days at the very least to give honor and glory to God's holy Name (Ps 28 LXX). Indeed it is obvious how great is the importance and virtue of assembling ourselves together in public prayer, since the Lord promised to be present Himself in the midst of such assemblies and to hear and receive our petitions (Matt 18:19–20). Consequently, whoever despises or neglects congregational prayer in the church deprives himself of the benefit of the Lord's most precious promise.

To awaken a disposition and to increase zeal to attend church for prayer, and especially to attend the celebration of the Holy Liturgy, we may derive great good from considering the following:

1. Examples in the word of God: Luke 2:37, Acts 3:1, Psalm 41:2–5 LXX, and Ps 83:2–3 LXX.
2. Examples in the lives of the Holy Fathers and ecclesiastical history, in which we read that the Christians of the early centuries showed such ardent zeal for their ecclesiastical assemblies and prayer that no persecutions, not even the fear of the most cruel forms of torture and death, could keep them away from attending church. And though in those times there were in some countries no public churches, they nevertheless met together on Sundays and other feast days in such places as they could to glorify God by the church service. For this we have the testimonies of the holy Martyr Justin and Tertullian in their "Apologies" besides other writers of the history of the Church.
3. The promises of God and the doctrine contained in many of the Psalms on this point ought to be a sufficient incitement both to the priest himself and to his parishioners.

When people do in fact attend the services of the Church in order that they may not risk losing the benefits of Christ's promises, the priest should explain to the common people that God's house "shall be called a house of prayer" (Matt 21:13) and that "in His temple doth every man [that attends] speak glory" (Ps 28:9 LXX). Consequently, those who stand in the church must stand with devotion and pay diligent attention to the reading of God's word and to all that is done or sung during the service to His glory. But in order to make all this edifying to those who attend, it is a most necessary part of the priest's duty to take care that the reader read intelligibly, according to that commandment which is written: "Do not be hasty with your mouth, And let not your heart be quick to utter a word before God" (Eccl 5:1 LXX). The same also is addressed to singers: "O sing unto our God, sing ye; ... with understanding" (Ps 46:7–8 LXX). Thus ordered, the reading and

singing will edify and comfort the hearer, and so the attention of
the ear will be followed by devotion of spirit.

"Walk carefully when you go to the house of God. And draw
near to hear" (Eccl 4:17 LXX). Here we should remind all that there
is nothing that can be done by him who stands in the church that is
more acceptable to God than to listen with attention to His word. The
prophet says the following: "If only the desired whole burnt offerings and desired sacrifices were equal to the Lord!, Behold!, Hearing is better than sacrifice and obedience than the fat of rams" (1 Kgs
15:22 LXX). The Holy Spirit Himself explains, through the words of
the Prophet Samuel, how great is the sin of not hearkening to God's
word, especially in the church, saying: "The sin is one and the same as
divination [witchcraft]. Idols bring grief and pain" (1 Kgs 15:23 LXX).

The very words of the proclamation that is so often made in the
church either by the priest or by the deacon: "Let us attend! Wisdom!
Let us attend!" should inspire all alike, singers, readers, and congregation, to earnest and devout attention.[49]

CHAPTER 15

Some Thoughts on Church Style and Its Effect on the Prayer of the Congregation

It is very important for a member of the clergy to fully feel the exalted nature of a church and the services performed therein. He must learn that just as anything secular is impermissible in regard to church utensils, artwork, paintings, and icons, so is it unacceptable in the services, sermons, and the appearance and behavior of the priest himself.

For example, any secular object brought into the church should immediately "cut" the eyes of the priest. Any nonreligious artistic depictions or singing of a secular, operatic character, ostentatious reading, exclamations, and even movements performed in a theatrical manner—all these should inspire protest from the congregation and even more so from the priest himself.

Of course, it is difficult to sustain a consistent, proper style in our churches. Our churches and services now have a very "mottled" character. Everything can be found in them—from ancient icons to Western reproductions and tastelessly affected photographs of pictures. Unsightly engraving, sculpture, artificial flowers, cumbersome bronze candle stands and chandeliers that have turned green, cloths with drab embroidery, frescoes of poor quality, worldly in character, inferior stained glass depictions—all these things fill our churches too often. At times there is an offensively little amount of taste and aesthetics. Certain depictions are nontraditional and appeared in comparatively recent times, such as the anthropomorphic depiction of God the Father, the painting of the "Agony in the Garden," the resurrected Saviour flying from the grave with a banner in hand, surrounded by angels and warriors, and depictions of a crowned Mother of God or depictions of the Mother of God with her head uncovered.

Similarly, reading and singing during the services are often an artificial combination of pieces eclectic in character and manner of performance. Much is sung in an operatic, secular fashion.

It is difficult to achieve strictness and a unified style in a church. Russians especially have grown used to garishness and sometimes we even like the miserable practice that has become so common. The priest needs to very carefully, very tactfully nurture in his parishioners an understanding of what is truly spiritual.

It is not the shouts from the choir (and they love to shout!) but the depth of content, the revelation of the meaning of the hymns, that is important and salvific. One can shout out or mumble through the Epistle or Gospel reading or one can convey it to the heart of a person praying. One can "be moved" by a poor copy of a Madonna or one can pray before an ancient grace-filled icon of the Mother of God and receive spiritual, not sensual, that is, superficial, comfort.

A lack of taste is especially evident among the manufacturers and buyers of miters. The abundance of glass, beads, brooches, and very poor depictions makes contemporary miters look theatrical and fake. It is a pity that the difference between episcopal and archimandrites' miters has been lost. Our mitered archpriests often do not even know how to wear miters, but wear them as bishops do. Unfortunately, crosses and panagias also do not always shine with taste. Manufacturers of ecclesiastical ware, unfortunately, often forget that there exist colors and materials that are altogether uncompatible. Besides, it is not the abundance of sparkle and imitation jewels but churchliness and beauty that make any ecclesial object appropriate to its high calling.

In our churches one can very frequently find a misuse of electricity. Often there are enormous chandeliers and reflecting surfaces that blind the congregation. Fluorescent lamps are also misused. At times the warm light from the oil lamps is replaced with lightbulbs. The church and services lose much due to this tasteless and constantly glaring electric lighting. It should be remembered that the eye of the modern man grows weary in everyday life from too much light, just as the ear does from daily noise.

Artificial flowers and garish ornaments are absolutely inadmissible in the church. Here everything must be special—ecclesiastical, to be exact. Here even the air is different—saturated with incense flowing in the sunbeams that penetrate the church. Can a lightbulb really take the place of a candle or an oil lamp—these symbols of living prayer and faith?

The church atmosphere must at all times be strict and exalted; here worldly effects are impermissible. In secular, realistic, and theatrical art much is built on illusion, but in the church there is no place for illusion. Here everything testifies to the reality and nearness of the spiritual realm; here the grace of Christ breathes and man prepares himself in church for its reception, purification, elevation, for drawing near to things sublime. The church is a spiritual house of healing, an exceptional place, the only such place on earth. A clergyman is obligated to keep this clearly in mind and to assist in the church's forever remaining a house of prayer.

The riches of spirit-bearing church art are boundless, and all of this is a testimony to Christ crucified and raised from the dead—in this is the everlasting life-creating power of the Church's depictive and monumental creativity. Perhaps the object most imbued with this power of the Church is the icon.

Orthodox icons can be seen everywhere—in homes and in museums as well as in churches. Copies of icons are printed in various publications and on greeting cards. Many have, as it were, "discovered icons," and they are loved and studied in various countries. However, it should always be remembered that the icon's true home is the church. There it becomes an icon in the full and perfect sense of the word. The icon, created by the Church, actively takes part in ecclesiastical life, helping the children of the Church to work out their salvation. Icons do not exist only to be admired or to serve as decorations but are for our salvation. Without prayer, spiritual life and drawing closer to God are impossible. Icons aid prayer; they nurture communion with God and a person's inner transfiguration.

Icons enlighten the entire life of the believer and, being always present before his bodily eyes, teach him to see and comprehend a world that is transcendent, spiritual, and eternal. It is for this reason that the ancient Orthodox icon does not in the least imitate the world, which is earthly, sensual, and temporal.

Opening up the spiritual world, the realm of faith, the icon heals man's restless spirit, indicating the one path to salvation—the Orthodox faith, the faith of the Church.

It is not human emotions and conjectures but the Church's centuries-old experience, its history and struggle, that are impressed in the icon; and they are impressed not as instances from ages past that have faded into history but as the eternally living breath of Christ's grace, as an expression of the eternal salvific truths of the faith, as the renewing power of the Risen Lord. The reality of the icon is the reality of the spiritual world and of His saving work here on earth. It is the reality of the salvation of every person striving toward salvation. Outside the Church, there are no icons. Outside the Church there are sculptures, paintings, engravings, photographs, gospel-themed films, and so forth. These are kinds of religious art.

The Orthodox icon is immeasurably higher than this art, because the icon is part of the life of the Orthodox Church—an essential part, directly relating to the very foundational dogmas of our faith. This was proven by the defenders of the holy icons at the Seventh Ecumenical Council. This is proven by the experience and history of the Church and every one of its members.

The illuminating action of the holy icon, the grace of God given in prayer before it according to faith, the striving of one's mind and heart toward the prototype—all these act on a person as a great blessing from God, as a gift, as an irreplaceable heavenly resource to Orthodox Christians living here on earth.

The words of the prayers, the peace of the church, and the services are always at one with the icon—they are a single whole. All the wealth of theology, all that has been attained by redeemed man on his path toward God is visibly reflected in the icons and in the churches' frescoes. All of this wealth will serve us as it has served and will continue to serve many generations on their path to salvation.

CONCLUDING THOUGHTS

An important aspect of a clergyman's life and work is his attitude toward holy things, toward his sacred office and colleagues, toward his duty, and his responsibilities toward his elders and his superiors. His attitude toward his family, toward those around him, toward mankind in general is a significant indicator of his spiritual wealth.

A clergyman should always be aided by the voice of his pastoral conscience, his strict inner supervisor. A strict, self-critical attitude toward one's behavior, toward one's knowledge and actions will help the clergyman to avoid lethargy, mistakes, complacency about one's achievements, carelessness, and sloth.

A pastor should have a constant, active sense of his duty and an awareness of his unworthiness. He should also be governed by a desire to overcome all difficulties with God's help, to do battle with his short-comings, to improve, to grow. Today a pastor is not a "preacher," not simply a formal rite-performer but a witness to Christ, a man serving the world while in the world. A pastor is a bearer of Christ's love to man; he is a person unlike all others, possessing all the best and highest traits of man and serving for the salvation of all people.

In church, at home, among people, an Orthodox clergyman is always one and the same—a dedicated, steadfast worker and, of course, an ascetic. Let no one be frightened by this word, for without spiritual struggle there is no Christianity; without spiritual struggle there cannot be priesthood either.

In general, what we have included here will suffice to give those who have not studied pastoral theology some notion of the pastoral duty and to inspire all, we may hope, with sincerity and zeal in this duty. And so now it is your turn, priests, to receive this treatise in a spirit of love and to read it through with diligent attention. The commandments of the Lord and the examples cited in it will act as inspiration, instruction, and confirmation in the doing of your duty. May the Holy Spirit Himself, the Spirit of truth, be in all things your Guide, Master, and Teacher.

"If you abide in Me, and My words abide in you, you will ask what you desire, and it shall be done for you" (John 15:7).

"Seeing then that we have a great High Priest who has passed through the heavens, Jesus the Son of God, let us hold fast our confession … Let us therefore come boldly to the throne of grace, that we may obtain mercy and find grace to help in time of need" (Heb 4:14–16).

"Let us draw near with a true heart in full assurance of faith, having our hearts sprinkled from an evil conscience and our bodies washed with pure water" (Heb 10:22).

Glory be to God.

NOTES

Introduction

1. Moses refused. Exodus iii. 11. iv. 13. and Jer. i. 6. So also in ancient times many refused and fled from this Order, as Gregory the Wonderworker of Neocaesarea, Ephraim the Syrian, Gregory the Divine, Ambrose, Augustine, Synesius, and many others, who were both by their lives and doctrines lights of the Church. St John Chrysostom on occasion of his fleeing the priesthood wrote his Six Books. How much more should they who are blinded by ignorance, by the darkness of vicious and impure lives, flee this Order?

Chapter 1: Instruction of the People by the Word

2. These Epistles under the names of Timothy and Titus are in reality addressed to all who bear the pastoral office therefore every one should have them written on the tablet of his heart and meditate upon them without ceasing by both day and night.
3. Canons of the Twelve Apostles, xxxvi.
4. Canons of the Twelve Apostles, lviii.
5. Canon VI of the Sixth Ecumenical Council.

Chapter 2: What and Where the Priest Should Teach

6. In English: Archpriest Seraphim Slobodskoy, Susan Price translated, *The Law of God* (Jordanville, NY: Holy Trinity Monastery, 1993); Archbishop Dmitri (Royster), *Orthodox Christian Teaching* (Brooklyn, OH: Orthodox Christian Publications Center, 1980); *Catechism of the Orthodox Church of St. Philaret* (Liberty, TN: St John of Kronstadt Press, 2009).
7. "So these words I command you today shall be in your heart and in our soul. You shall teach them to your sons" (Deut 6:6, 7). "You shall speak My words to them" (Ezek 2:7). "Hear a word from My mouth, and shall threaten them from Me" (Ezek 3:17).
8. The nineteenth canon of the Sixth Ecumenical Council orders that the people be instructed in the true faith out of Holy Scripture. To the same purpose is Canon XVI of the Council of Laodicea.

9. "Blessed are they that search into His testimonies, with their whole heart shall they seek Him" (Ps 119:2). See also (Acts 17:2) and (1 Tim 6:3, 4), as well as the parables of the treasure hid in the field and of the pearl of great price (Matt 13:44, 45, 46).

10. St Ambrose, lib. iii. De Fide, ch. Vii; Dionysius the Areopagite, in Divine Hierarchy, ch. I; Canon lxxxv. of those attributed to the Apostles; Canon lviii. of the Council of Laodicea, according to the Nomocanon, and Canon xxiv., according to the Nomocanon, of the Council of Carthage enumerate the books of the Old and New Testaments and give them the name of Divine Scripture, and the above-mentioned canon of the Council of Carthage runs thus: "Let nothing besides the books named in the Canons, be reckoned in the Church under the name of Divine Scripture."

11. For a more detailed description of the process of Scripture's canonization, read the introductory section of Archbishop Averky (Taushev)'s *Commentary on the Four Gospels*, available from Holy Trinity Publications.

12. Church Tradition includes canons and constitutions by which is defined how the ecclesiastical community is to be governed, what feasts are to be kept to the glory of God, when, and with what observances. Fasting again is by the Lord's own commandment: but when to keep fast and when not, and with what distinctions of food, this we have from tradition. Briefly, the whole body of Orders, Services, and Sacraments of the Church, the principle of which we have in the word of God is called, and is indeed part of, Church Tradition.

13. See the Prologue (or Book of Homilies) for the month of August, Day xvii.

14. See the Prologue, August xviii.

Chapter 3: How the Priest Should Teach

15. An allusion to the liturgical prayer: "O Heavenly King, Comforter, Spirit of Truth … " Prayer Book, Fourth Edition—Revised (Jordanville, New York: Holy Trinity Publications, 2003).

16. Augustine, Epist. lxi. to the Bishop Aurelius, writes thus: "Let a man forbid and hinder with mildness what he can; but what he cannot, let him bear with patience, sighing and weeping with tears of charity."

17. On this point also, see Chrysostom's sixth homily on 2 Timothy.

18. For more on the subject of this difficulty and the need for caution, see the same book, chapters 3 and 4.

19. Chrysostom, on 2 Tim., Hom. ix., writes thus: "What is 'in season'? It is this: Have no limited time: have time always: not only in peace and ease; nor only when you sit in the church; but also in danger itself: though you are shut up in prison, or clapped with irons: though you are already condemned, and leading to death: even then reprove, and cease not to rebuke: for then only will it be no season to rebuke, when your reproof will have had effect."

Chapter 4: On Instruction by Deed

20. The abbreviation of *Strōmateis*, literally "Miscellanies."

21. *Sober-minded*, in Greek Σώφρων, means, as St John Chrysostom explains it in his twentieth homily on Romans, a man who has a sound mind, with which the word used in the Russian version agrees, meaning a man of sound sense or reason, neither distorted nor defective.

22. Apostolic Canon XXV, Canons I and IX of Neocaesarea, and Canon III of St Basil.

23. Canon VIII of Neocaesarea and Canon XXVIII of St Basil.

24. Canon III of the First Ecumenical Council, Canon V of the Sixth Ecumenical Council, Canon XVIII of the Seventh Ecumenical Council, and Decree LXXI of Justinian vii.

25. Canon XVI of the Seventh Ecumenical Council.

26. Buffoonery is forbidden under pain of deposition by Apostolic Canon XLIII and Canon LI of the Sixth Ecumenical Council. Priests are to leave companies where there is dancing or playing, according to Canon XXIV of the Sixth Ecumenical Council and by Canon LIII of the Council of Laodicea.

27. St John Chrysostom, explaining the word *hospitable* in his second sermon on Titus, says the following: "He is given to hospitality, who makes himself a sharer in all that he has with the poor."

28. See Apostolic Canon LIX and Council of Laodicea VIII.

29. Apostolic Canon XLIII has the following: "Let any bishop, priest, or deacon who plays cards or drinks, unless he leave it off, be suspended." Apostolic Canon LIV: "Let the clergyman who without any necessity frequents taverns be excommunicated." Canon XXIV of the Council of Laodicea.

30. Apostolic Canon XXVI and Canon LV of St Basil the Great order that a priest who strikes any man, whether believer or unbeliever, be suspended.

31. In the Russian version in 1 Timothy 3:3, there is a word, which we have translated as *greedy*, while in the Epistle to Titus chapter 1:7 there is another, which the KJV has translated *a lover of filthy lucre:* but in the original Greek there is only one word, αἰσχροκερδής, which in both places denotes a man who makes sinful gains: and so *greediness* and *the love of filthy lucre* are two names for the same thing, the seeking of improper gain, which may be done in various ways unbecoming of the priesthood.

32. See also 1 Pet 5:2 and 1 Thess 2:5.

33. Apostolic Canon XLIV, Canon XVI of the First Ecumenical Council, Canon 10 of the Sixth Ecumenical Council.

34. Canon XIV of the Fourth Ecumenical Council and Canon XXXVI of the Council of Carthage.

35. Concerning the religious bringing up of children, see Canon XXXV of the Council of Carthage.

36. Luke 22:24; 1 Pet. 5:2; and 2 Corinth. 1:24.

Chapter 5: On the Sacraments in General

37. Preach the Gospel to every creature. "He who believes and is baptized will be saved; but he who does not believe will be condemned" (Mark 16:16). "He who believes in Him is not condemned; but he who does not believeth is condemned already, because he has not believed in the name of the only begotten Son of God" (John 3:18).

38. Canon XXIII of the Sixth Ecumenical Council has these words: "If the Priest who communicates the people in the all-pure Mysteries, that is, the all-pure Body and all-pure Blood of our Lord Jesus Christ, asks so much as a farthing, or any thing else whatever from the communicant, let him be suspended."

Chapter 6: Some Important Aspects of Each Sacrament in Particular, Beginning with the Sacrament of Holy Baptism

39. Canon LXXVIII of the Council in Trullo has these words: "Let him who seeks to be illuminated by Holy Baptism, be made to confess the faith." And the Gloss: "It is requisite that he who comes to Divine Baptism should learn the faith; that is, to repeat, 'I believe in one God' and recite this Creed before the bishop or before the priests. On the same subject, see Canon XLV of the Council of Laodicea.

40. See Canon XLVI of the same council and Canon XLV of the Council of Carthage.

41. Canon XXI of the Council of Ancyra, Canon XXI of the Sixth Ecumenical Council, and Canon XCI of St Basil the Great.

42. See Canons LXXXIII of Carthage and LXXXV of the Sixth Ecumenical Council.

Chapter 8: The Sacrament of Confession

43. See Canon XIII of the First Ecumenical Council and Canon VII of Carthage and Canon V of St Gregory of Nyssa.

Chapter 9: The Sacrament of Holy Communion and Some General Remarks Regarding the Serving of the Divine Liturgy

44. St John Chrysostom. Sermon twenty-seven on 1 Corinthians 13:27.

45. On the same subject, see also his twenty-fourth moral on 1 Corinthians and his seventeenth moral on Hebrews.

Chapter 10: The Sacrament of Matrimony

46. In the Nomocanon read what is said of marriage at fol. dxxi.

47. The text here refers to Russian prerevolutionary law. In any case, the priest must be acquainted with the civil matrimonial law of his state and/or country.

Chapter 13: How to Pray in Spirit and Truth

48. *The Divine Liturgy of Our Father among the Saints John Chrysostom: Slavonic-English Parallel Text* 3rd edition (Jordanville, NY: Holy Trinity Publications, 2015), 169.

Chapter 14: Prayer as the Special Duty of Priests

49. On standing and listening in church, see St John Chrysostom's nineteenth moral on Acts, his thirty-first homily on 1 Corinthians, his thirty-sixth moral on 2 Thessalonians, and his third and fifteenth morals on Hebrews.

SUBJECT INDEX

Aaron   x, 29, 151, 156
abomination   125, 150
Abraham   131
absolution   83–4, 86–7, 89, 92, 95–6,
    98, 115
abstinence   64, 141, 143
admonition   20, 25, 27, 95
adulterers   18, 96
adultery   37, 39–40, 90, 111
adversities   18, 40, 111, 157
afflictions   24, 66, 158
Alexei I of Moscow and All
    Russia   vii
alms   41, 95, 101, 123, 159
altar   xiv, 3, 42, 45, 56, 74, 100,
    103–6, 108–9, 154, 156, 162–3
Ambrose, St   12, 87, 174
    "On Faith"   11
    first book on repentance   86
Amphilochius, Bishop of Iconium, St,
    Iambics to Seleucius   12
angels xiv–xvi,   4, 12, 90, 102, 109,
    131, 140, 168
anointing   27, 74, 81
Apostolic Canon   59, 61, 175
    XLIII   175
    XLIV   175
    XVIII   61
    XXIX   59
    XXV   175
    XXVI   175
    LIV   175

Athanasius the Great, St
    commentary on the parables of the
        Gospels   87
    Epistles on the Feasts   11–12
Augustine, Blessed   173–4
    on Christian Doctrine   56
    Commentary on the Gospel of St.
        John   19
    De Dogma Ecclesia   95
    on sinful living   20
    sermon CCXXII   77
    sixteenth sermon on the lord's
        discourses   98
    treatise On the Departed
        132

baptism   xiii, xiv
    articles of faith   77–80
    Catechism, explanation   79
    grace and power of   78
    by layperson   78
    rebaptism   78
Basil the Great, St   131
    Canon III   175
    Canon XXVIII   175
    Canon XXXIV   96
    Canon LV   175
    Canons from New Testament
        (Part LXX)   153
    the Divine Liturgy of   163
    on Divine Services   100
    first sermon on fasting   142

on Lord's commandments and
traditions   14
Morals, Canon   72, 11–12
prayers for the Day of
Pentecost   159
Short Canons   11
believers   35–6, 123, 152, 169, 175
Bible   28. *See also* Scripture
birth   5, 25, 78, 104
bishop   xiii–xiv, 3, 5, 35, 38–9, 48,
50, 53, 78, 81, 101, 103, 108–9,
112–13, 175–6
bless   42, 58, 95, 107–8, 115, 130, 136,
140, 164
blessings   57, 74, 106–8, 134–6, 138
blood   4, 31, 94, 150, 163
of Christ   72, 90, 92–4, 96, 99–102,
116, 162–3, 176
bribes   60, 154
burial   105, 107, 131

calamities   147, 155
canonical sanction   59, 113
Canon III   175
Canon VI   173
Canon VII   176
Canon VIII   175
Canon IX   59
Canon XLV   176
Canon XLVI   176
Canon LI   175
Canon LIII   175
Canon LV   175
Canon LIX   78
Canon LXVI   19
Canon LXVIII   78
Canon LXXII   12
Canon LXXVIII   176
Canons LXXXIII of Carthage   176
Canons LXXXV   174, 176
Canon XCI   176
Canon CII   96

catechisms   79, 164, 173
caution   19, 24, 161, 174
ceremonies   78, 113
pagan   112
charity   14, 22, 36, 143, 174
children   26–7, 29, 60–2, 77, 80–1,
88, 111–13, 136–7, 142–3, 150–1,
154, 160, 164, 169, 175
baptizing   77
spiritual   47, 160
chrism   71, 81, 105
chrismation   71, 81
Christians   10, 24–5, 41, 52, 72, 78, 96,
112–13, 126, 143, 145–6, 164–5
exhorting   9
single union (family)   63
true   91
church   12–14, 18–22, 26–31, 34–5,
38–9, 43–5, 49–51, 59–65, 78–81,
103–6, 112, 123, 159–60, 164–71,
173–4
Clement of Alexandria
Instructor, The (first and second
book)   143
Stroma   35
Stromata (second book)   86
clergyman/men   28, 33–4, 38, 42–7,
49, 51–4, 56, 60–3, 75, 103–8, 169,
171, 175
commemoration   27, 102, 108, 159–60
commune   92, 99–100, 102–3
communion   27, 78, 89, 91–2, 94, 96,
98–100, 102–3, 109, 162–3. *See
also* Holy Communion
companions   47, 51, 54, 63
compassion   5, 22, 25
condemnation   17, 36–8, 64, 86, 99,
101, 117, 126, 143, 161
confession   21, 27, 65, 81, 83–9, 91, 93,
95, 97–8, 102, 109, 143, 150, 172, 176
after   97
at the time of   88

before 83–8
fasting periods 83–4
kinds and distinctions of sins 89
nature of explanation 87
public 88
true repentance 83–4
without faith 86
confessor 21, 79, 94, 98, 102
congregation 41–2, 93, 100, 108,
    112, 123, 142, 151, 160, 166–8
conscience 24, 33, 56, 85, 89, 100–1,
    109
consent 55, 113
consolation 24, 115
contrition 126, 143, 148, 156
conversation 27, 36, 51, 54–5, 104, 163
conversion 13, 18, 20, 71
Council of Ancyra 176
Council of Carthage 19, 50, 174–6
    Canon XXXV 175
    Canon XXXVI 175
    Canon LXVI 19
Council of Laodicea 173–6
    Canon VIII 175
    Canon XXIV 175
    Canon LIII 175
Council of Neo-Caesarea orders 39
Councils of Nicaea and
    Constantinople 10
covetousness 17, 36, 58–9, 95, 145, 158
creation 13, 61, 123
Creator 49, 111, 150
Creed (The Symbol of Faith) 10, 72,
    77, 108, 112, 176

dangers xv–xvi, 18–19, 27, 31, 42,
    47, 53, 60, 81, 98, 147, 158, 161,
    174
Daniel 156, 163
darkness 26, 90, 135, 173
David, the Prophet 28, 90, 117, 125,
    131, 156

deacons 28, 41–3, 65, 163, 166,
    175
death 10, 21, 25, 39, 81, 88, 90, 98–9,
    115–16, 131, 139, 154–5, 158, 165,
    174
Decree LXXI 175
deeds 11, 26, 36, 38, 40
degrees 96, 112
deliverance 21, 84, 137, 142
despair 15, 20, 23–4, 86, 88, 90
destruction 10, 97, 144, 149
devil 19, 24, 38, 40, 64–5, 93, 137,
    142, 147
devotion 16, 41, 56, 74, 122, 126,
    129–30, 157, 162–3, 165–6
Didymus of Alexandria 35
dignity xv–xvi, 44–5, 50–2, 93
diligence 18, 48, 83, 139, 164
Dionysius the Areopagite, St 12,
    174
    Divine Hierarchy 11
disciples xiii, 21–2, 30, 34–7, 93, 125,
    142, 151
discipline 13, 20, 34–5, 47, 66, 158
diseases 20, 27, 57, 83, 91, 115
dispositions 74, 88, 130, 165
doctrine 7, 9–12, 14–15, 25–6, 29,
    35, 38, 57, 64, 68, 73, 165
    soul-destroying 18–19
    superstitious 15
dominion 21, 135, 154
Donatists 19
drinking 38, 40, 54, 56, 68, 85
drunkards 56–7, 96
drunkenness 40, 57, 95, 140, 144–5

ecclesiastical 123, 141, 165, 169
edification 17, 36, 73, 97
elders 5, 54–5, 140, 152, 171
enemies 21, 106, 137, 140, 154–5
Ephesus 3, 31, 151–2
eternity 89, 134

Eucharist   74, 99. *See also*
    communion; Holy Communion
  Canon   108–9
  Holy Mysteries   64, 92, 98, 101–2,
    109, 163
evils   22, 25, 38, 41, 56, 58–9, 61, 87,
    90–1, 129–30, 141–2, 144–5, 147,
    150, 154–5

faith   9–10, 12–17, 23–4, 26, 34–6,
    59–61, 65, 71–3, 77–9, 86,
    113, 115–16, 122–3, 131–3,
    169–70
  holy   10, 24–5, 30, 64, 123, 153
fasting   14, 85, 95, 140–5, 148, 150,
    156, 174
faults   24, 58, 84–5, 94, 126
fear   52, 56, 58, 72–3, 84, 93, 100,
    102–4, 107, 122–3, 126, 148, 158,
    161–3, 165
feast days   31, 63, 123, 160, 164–5
First Ecumenical Council   175
  Canon III   175
  Canon VII of Carthage   176
  Canon XII   96
  Canon XVI   175
  Canon CII   96
flesh   xv, 24, 40, 67, 73, 84, 89, 102,
    129, 131, 137, 160–2
flock   xv, 4–5, 9, 15–16, 35, 39, 42,
    54, 60, 65, 74, 93
food   7, 14, 50, 53–4, 68, 74, 133, 141,
    147, 174
forgiveness   87, 91, 136, 146, 148,
    154–5
fornication   39–40, 95, 111, 158
fourth Council of Carthage
  Canon XV   50
Fourth Ecumenical Council
  Canon XIV   175
fullness   xiv, 22, 104, 108, 121, 130,
    144

gifts   60, 71, 101, 116, 122, 123, 130,
    134–5, 155, 170
  Holy Gifts   59, 92, 162–3
  spiritual   133, 135, 148
  supernatural   157
  temporal   133, 147
glory   xiii–xiv, 17–19, 23, 31, 53, 57,
    102, 123, 125, 130, 133–7, 150,
    157, 163–5, 172
  everlasting   117
God   xiii–xiv, 3–7, 9–19, 23–31,
    33–8, 56–60, 66–8, 71–3, 77–80,
    84–98, 115–17, 121–7, 129–50,
    152–61, 163–74. *See also* Jesus,
    Christ
  glory   17, 123, 130, 143, 174
  Holy Spirit   xiii, xv, 7, 11–13, 39,
    41, 78–9, 91, 93, 99–101, 132–3,
    135, 145–7, 150, 159–62
  Holy Trinity   10, 72, 78
  house of   67, 104, 166
  inward and outward service
    of   122–3, 125–6
  wisdom of   4, 26
  wrath of   21, 85
gospel   3, 5–6, 9, 12, 17, 19, 25–6, 28,
    31, 34, 36, 71–4, 87, 135, 152–3
grace   xiii–xiv, 4, 72–3, 78–9, 81,
    90–3, 98–9, 103, 116, 124, 126,
    135, 139, 169–70, 172
grave   28, 107, 167
Gregory the Theologian, St.   12, 98,
    173
  Eighth Sermon on Ephesians   18
  First Oration   5
  twenty-fourth epistle   98
grief   6, 24, 166
guests   5, 55
guide   7, 11, 23, 30, 60, 133, 135, 155,
    172
guilty   xvi, 7, 23, 73, 101, 103, 113,
    126, 162

habits   34, 63, 86, 91–2, 95, 107
Hannah   124
harmony   45, 108
healing   7, 115, 143, 169
health   7, 27, 52, 111, 133, 136, 141,
    155, 160
hearers   16–18, 21–2, 33, 35, 57, 166
hearing   37, 71, 109, 123, 149, 166
heaven   21, 23, 25, 34, 99–101, 103,
    121, 123, 131, 135, 137–8, 140,
    152, 154, 156
hell   20–1, 89, 158
heretics   18–19, 73, 81
history   47, 49, 106, 112, 165, 170
    ecclesiastical   28, 56, 165
holiness   23, 33, 102, 104–5, 130, 134,
    154
holy
    crosses   105
    objects   64, 105
    water   64, 103
Holy Communion   98–9, 101, 103,
    105, 107, 109, 176
    altar, cleanliness and neatness   106
    blessing during services   107
    bows and kneeling   107
    censing   107
    Divine Liturgy context   103,
        107–8
    Divine Mysteries   109, 160
    Eucharistic Canon   109
    hierarchical service   108
    inappropriate behavior   104
    preparations for   100
    sacred objects   105
    to sick   109
    signing the cross   106–7
Holy Fathers   5, 9, 11, 13–14, 18, 28,
    40, 50, 56, 59, 141, 152, 165
honor   17–18, 24, 31, 51, 54, 93, 97,
    102, 126, 129–30, 133–4, 137, 157,
    159, 164

hospitality   53, 63, 175
household   41, 55, 60–3, 68, 143, 150
humble   22, 25, 37, 64, 141, 143
humility   14, 19, 31, 64, 67, 97, 101,
    104, 122–3, 145, 148, 163
hypocrisy   44, 68, 125, 145
hypocrites   4, 33, 36, 68, 125, 149

icons   38, 61–2, 64, 103, 106–7, 167,
    169–70
Ignatius the God-bearer, St, Epistle to
    the holy martyr Polycarp   22
immortal   129, 137
impure   73, 154, 173
impurity   71, 73, 129, 158
incense   16, 150, 169
injunctions   66, 79, 85, 132–3, 140,
    159
intercession   133, 146, 151
intercessors   155
interests   46, 49, 51, 53, 59, 62–4
    clergyman's range of   46–7
Isaiah, Prophet   6, 149

Jerome, St
    second epistle to Nepotianus   38,
        53, 60
    sixth moral on Leviticus VIII   29
Jesus, Christ   xiii–xiv, xvi–xvii, 86,
    95–7, 99–103, 124, 130–1, 136–7
    Body and Blood of Christ   96, 99,
        101–2
    and David on prayer   125
    Epistle to the Ephesians 2:
        8–10   17
    on good pastorship   34–5
    His Last and Mystical Supper   160
    on Holy Communion   99
    on Holy Spirit   11
    Incarnation of   13
    instruction for prayer   133–7
    judgment of   6, 30, 100

Salvific faith   72
Tabernacle of Witness   73
on teaching and preaching   3–4
Jews   9, 11, 30–1, 66, 71, 99, 101
John the Baptist   35, 96
John Chrysostom, St   55–6, 65
   on clergymen's marriage   39
   on confession   87
   Eighth Sermon on Ephesians   18
   eighty-third sermon on
      Matthew   92, 101
   Epistle to the Romans   6
   Epistle to Titus   5
   fifteenth moral on 2
      Corinthians   160
   fifth homily on 2 Thessalonian   34
   first homily on Acts   36
   first homily on Genesis   144
   first sermon on Genesis   141
   forty-first moral on 1
      Corinthians   159
   forty-fourth moral on Acts 20   65
   fourteenth moral on   2
      Corinthians   96
   fourth moral on   2
      Thessalonians   160
   fourth sermon on Genesis   144
   Galatians   21
   on hospitality   175
   kinds and distinctions of sins   91
   nineteenth homily on
      Ephesians   158
   On the Priesthood   17, 20, 30, 109,
      159, 161–2
   second homily on Romans   160
   second moral on Titus   40, 61
   sermon on the Blessed
      Philogonus   96, 101
   sermon on the fall of first man   98
   seventy-second sermon on
      Matthew   37
   sixth homily on 2 Timothy.   174

sixth homily on Timothy   152
sixth moral on 1 Timothy   23
sixth sermon on Romans   37
on sober-mindedness   175
on strikers   58
tenth homily on Matthew   27
tenth moral on Matthew   95
third book on the priesthood   40
third moral on Acts   110
third moral on Ephesians   102
third moral on Philippians   159
thirtieth moral on Acts   37
thirty-fourth homily on
   Hebrews   27
thirty-fourth homily on
   Hebrews   22
twelfth homily on Philippians   67
twelfth moral on Colossians   112
twenty-eighth homily on 2
   Corinthians   22
twenty-second moral on
   Hebrews   84
John of Damascus, St
   Faith (fourth book)   12
   Parallels   35
   treatise on icons   38
Judas   59, 86, 93
judgment   xvi, 3, 6, 17, 21, 30,
   88–9, 100, 142, 145, 153–6, 160,
   162
justification   10, 58, 66, 100, 115,
   131
Justin the Martyr, St   165
   Decree LXXI   175
   fortieth Question   86

kingdom   xvi, 34, 56, 117, 131,
   134–5, 137–8, 148
kneeling   107, 127, 153
knowledge   4, 9, 16, 18, 24–8, 34,
   46–7, 49, 51–3, 63–4, 71–2, 130,
   133, 135, 157

laborers xv, 152

labors xv, 6, 17–18, 22, 31, 52, 62–3, 66–7, 126, 136–7, 139–40, 145, 154, 164

lambs xvi, 26, 103

law 4, 6, 9–10, 14, 17, 25, 29–30, 37, 39, 77, 79, 84, 121–2, 133, 139

life 22–3, 26, 28–9, 33–4, 36–8, 46–8, 52–3, 56, 62–4, 91, 103, 130–2, 134–6, 144–5

  eternal xiv, 25, 59, 99, 137

  everlasting xiii, 10, 23, 109, 116

  everyday 63, 168

  holy xvi–xvii, 35, 72, 153

  temporal 116, 138, 157

  virtuous 35, 86, 95, 139

liturgy 74, 159

  Divine Liturgy 62, 99–100, 103, 107–9, 160, 163, 176–7

love 22–4, 33–5, 51–2, 58–61, 63–4, 77, 79–80, 116–17, 122–3, 126, 130–1, 133–5, 140, 145, 157–8

lust 18, 25, 87, 90, 112, 144

Macarius, St, *On Keeping the Heart* 132, 145

malice 98, 145

Manasseh 90, 133

mankind xiii, 19, 24, 111, 116, 140–2, 171

marriage 111–13, 176

Marcellinus, Ammianus 50

matrimony 111–13, 176

Mediator 115, 146, 163

meditations 126, 130–1, 133

Methodius, Patriarch of Constantinople, Nomocanon 94

ministers xiv, 3, 53, 68, 73, 97, 142, 161–3

Mogila, Peter, Euchologion 79

money 38, 53, 58–9, 74

morals 11–12, 27, 177

  good xvi

mortal 129, 133

Moses 13, 29, 124, 155–6, 163, 173

mysteries 10, 93, 102, 104, 112, 160–2

  all-pure 176

  of God xvii, 159

Mystical Supper 152, 160

neatness 46, 63, 106

neglect 14, 28, 37, 52, 125, 144, 147–8

  to pray 147–8, 150

negligence 5, 27, 78–9, 88, 93, 109

neighbors xvi, 25, 33, 57, 94, 122–3, 143, 148–9

Nepotian 38, 53, 60

New Testament xiii, 4, 9–13, 28, 56, 73, 92, 140, 142–3, 151, 153, 160, 174

Nicodemus, St 59

Nomocanon 78, 94, 112, 174, 176

oath 65, 90

obedience 19, 34, 122–3, 135, 137, 166

oblations 103, 108, 159

offerings 16, 74, 123, 166

oil lamps 62–3, 168–9

Old church objects 105–6

Old Testament xvii, 10, 56, 60, 73, 91, 141–2, 158

  Church 151

  Levitical books 140

oral prayer 125–6, 132

ordinance 56, 141, 151

ordination 44, 51, 59, 75, 109

Paganism 78, 112, 121

pain 4, 56, 59, 88, 158, 166, 175

  sharpest 98

parishioners   1, 5–6, 10, 15–17, 23, 26–7, 30, 53, 64–5, 74, 78, 83–4, 87–8, 165, 168
Parthenius (Sopkovsky) Bishop   vii
pastor. *See* priests
Paul, Apostle   3, 5, 9, 12, 17, 21–2, 26, 29–30, 34–6, 38–9, 59–60, 64, 66–8, 72, 90, 152–3, 160
    on drinkards   56
    on evangelical patience   58
    on faith   71
    fifth homily on   1 Timothy   36
    instructions to Timothy   151
    on prayer   124, 130, 140
    tenth homily   36
    thirteenth homily   36
    on Unction   116
penances   21, 78–9, 92, 94–6, 98
penitence   87, 93–5
Philaret, St.   173
Philogonus, Blessed   96, 101
prayers   41–2, 61–3, 65, 74, 84, 87, 89, 100–1, 119, 129–34, 136–55, 157–65, 167, 169–70
    dead, for the   159
    inward and outward service of God   122–3, 125–6
    natural reason   123
    preparation   126
    priest's duties   122–3
    private   123–6
    public   123, 126
    purpose   121
    without ceasing   ix, 157, 173
praying in Sprit and truth
    inward   132
    motives and incitements   146
    oral   132
    private   129
    public   129
preacher   3, 17–18, 26, 33–4, 45, 98, 171

preaching   xiii–xiv, 5, 9, 13, 17–18, 33, 36, 71–2, 123, 152–3
priests   xiii–xvi. *See also specific services*
    ability to listen   49–50
    alcoholism   56–7
    appearance and behavior   41, 43–6, 50, 63–4
    bribing   60
    examination of sins   91
    examples of teaching   16–17
    family life   63–4
    feast day celebration   64
    fivefold distinction, teachings   15
    holy living, need for   60–2
    hospitality   53–5
    industriousness   52
    infatuations   65
    interest in church antiquity   49
    Liturgy preparation   62–3
    orderliness   62
    personal culture   46–9, 54–5, 61–2
    self-education   47–8
    self-will, or undue self-love   64
    socialization   50
    speech   51
    unlawful gain   58–9, 66
priesthood   xiii–xvi, 4, 6, 17–18, 20, 28, 30, 39–41, 65, 67, 151–2, 159, 161–3, 171, 173
    duty of prayer   41–2
    giving way to sensual pleasures   39
    serving habits   42–3, 63
prophets   xiii, 4, 13, 21, 38, 66, 123, 125, 144, 156, 161, 166. *See also individual prophets*
    false xvi,   12
prosperity   111, 158
prosperous   29, 158
prostrations   78, 107, 127
providence   56, 134, 139

provider   49, 104, 121, 134

punishment   37, 60, 85, 100, 110, 132, 142, 156

purification   98, 141, 143, 169

purify   93, 158, 161

purity   35–6, 40, 77, 100, 102, 122–3, 142, 161–2

quarrels   57, 87, 143

rank   xiv, 44, 48, 52

reading   13, 29, 43, 46–9, 62, 64, 105, 108–9, 123, 162, 165, 167–8

remission   25, 84, 86, 123, 133, 136

repentance   9–10, 23–5, 30, 84–8, 90, 92, 95–7, 102, 116, 123, 133, 136, 143, 150, 155
  true   21, 83–4, 86, 91–2, 97, 109, 115–16, 141, 143, 150

responsibilities   37, 65, 83, 104, 109, 171

resurrection   13, 26, 109, 131, 159

revelation   12, 123, 145, 168

reverence   33, 35, 38, 41, 60, 100, 106–7, 111, 153, 162

righteousness   7, 15, 24–5, 59, 139, 143, 154

Sabbaths   x, 150

Sacraments xvi,   3, 5, 68–9, 71–5, 77–9, 81, 83, 85, 87, 99–100, 102–3, 111–13, 115, 176. *See also* Unction

sacrifice xiv,   16, 41, 79, 95, 116, 123, 148, 161–2, 166

saints, xiv   102, 140, 150. *See also individual saints*

salvation   4–7, 9–11, 16–20, 23–4, 27–8, 30, 34, 60, 72, 90, 97, 101, 110, 115–16, 169–1
  everlasting   xiv, 25, 135, 147

Samuel, Prophet   124, 166

sanctification   25, 136, 144

Saturdays   63

Scripture   xiii, xv, 7, 9–12, 15, 28–30, 38, 73, 132, 138, 144, 159, 161

sermon   13–14, 17–18, 56, 65, 167

services   33–4, 41–5, 47–8, 52, 59, 62–3, 65, 103–5, 107–8, 122–3, 150–1, 160–2, 165, 167–8, 170

Service of Thanksgiving. *See* Holy Communion

Seventh Ecumenical Council   30, 170, 175
  Canon XVI   175
  Canon XVIII   175

severity   20, 88, 160

shame   11, 46, 88, 144

shepherds   xiv, xvi, 4, 6–7, 35, 154, 157

shortcomings   42, 171

sicknesses   52, 88, 111, 115, 158

sincerity   63, 104, 112, 145, 171

sinful/sinfulness   24, 33, 43, 52, 85, 87, 95–6, 112, 133, 136

sinners   xiii–xiv, 20–2, 26, 85, 89–92, 94, 116–17, 142

sins   15–16, 20–2, 25–7, 57–8, 72–3, 83–100, 115, 125–6, 129, 132–3, 135–9, 143–4, 146–7, 154–6, 159–60

Sixth Ecumenical Council
  Canon V   175
  Canon XXIII   59
  Canon XXIV   175
  Canon CII   96
  Canon LI   175
  Canon LIX   78

sobriety   40, 140, 142, 144–5, 148, 161

souls   18, 20, 25, 27–30, 38–9, 57–8, 83, 85–6, 91–2, 101–2, 124–6, 129–33, 141–3, 158, 161–3

speech   xvi, 46, 48–9
  cultured   49
  enriches   51

everyday   48
  priest's   51
  sound   35
  unctuous   64
speech defect   42
Statutes   33, 37–8, 141
stewards/stewardship   xvii, 4, 68, 159
  perfect   67
  wise   67

teachers   xiii–xv, 11–12, 18, 20–1, 28, 33, 35–9, 58, 61, 65, 133, 153, 172
teaching   xiii, xvi, 3, 6, 11, 15–16, 18–19, 22–4, 26, 30, 36–8, 67
  with actions   37–8, 41
  fivefold distinction   15–31
  great   31
  Lord's commandments and traditions   13–14, 174 n.12
  rule for   33–5
  what and where   9–14
temperance   14, 38, 40, 50, 143
temptations   24–5, 39, 50, 137, 147, 151
tenets   9–10, 13–14, 16–17
Tertullian   90, 165
testimonies   11–12, 56, 65, 79, 143, 156, 159, 161, 165, 169, 174
thanksgiving   41, 99, 122, 141, 146, 150, 158–9, 164
thief   xvi, 53, 90, 117, 138, 144
traditions   13–14, 43, 54, 63, 174
transgressions   21, 24–5, 91, 94, 116, 135, 159
treatise   38, 132, 172
trust   79, 84, 86, 88–9, 115–17, 122–4, 130
truth   7, 10–11, 25–6, 122–7, 129–33, 135, 137, 139, 141, 143, 145–50, 152, 163–4, 172, 174
  divine   10
  dogmatic   9
  strictest   xv

Unction
  priest's duty   115
  use of passages   116–17
unrighteousness   4, 129, 143, 147, 155

vain   6, 139, 145, 150, 159
veneration   104, 107
vengeance   26, 84
vessels   97, 105, 144, 146
vigilance   37, 39–40, 62, 144
virginity   145–6
vows   65, 77, 79

war   24–5, 74, 87, 155
weaknesses   22, 33, 39, 53–4, 85, 133, 146
wealth   49, 170
wedding   5, 146
widows   39, 53, 61
wife   38–40, 60, 63, 111
wine   22, 38, 54, 56–7, 99, 109, 144
wisdom   13, 25–6, 28–9, 45, 67–8, 121–2, 166
witness   11, 17, 30, 34, 56, 73, 97, 104, 107, 146, 171
woman/women   27, 41, 65, 77–9, 112, 113
worship   16, 41, 65, 122–4, 127, 142, 150
worshippers true   50, 124, 129
wound   20, 22, 57, 84–5, 89, 96, 98
wrath   21, 84–5, 89, 142, 144, 148, 156, 158

Zechariah, Prophet   144
zealous xvi,   125, 142, 153, 164

SCRIPTURE INDEX

The Old Testament

Baruch 3:4–5, p. 159

Daniel 2:21, p. 136
Daniel 10:9, p. 163
Deuteronomy 1:13, p. 153
Deuteronomy 1:16–17, p. 154
Deuteronomy 4:9, p. 29
Deuteronomy 15:9, p. 25
Deuteronomy 16:19, p. 154
Deuteronomy 27:26, p. 85

Ecclesiastes 4:17 LXX, p. 166
Ecclesiastes 5:1 LXX, p. 132, 165

1 Esdras 9, p. 156

Exodus 14:15, p. 124
Exodus 17, p. 155
Exodus 17:14, p. 13
Exodus 18:21, p. 153
Exodus 19:22, p. 161
Exodus 20:17, p. 25
Exodus 30:19–21, p. 73
Exodus 30:20, p. 161
Exodus 32:11, p. 156
Exodus 40:31, p. 73
Ezekiel 1:28, p. 163
Ezekiel 3:17–18, p. 4
Ezekiel 7–9, p. 66
Ezekiel 13:3, p. 66

Ezekiel 18: 30, p. 156
Ezekiel 22:30–31, p. 156
Ezekiel 33:11, p. 90, 116
Ezekiel 33:7, p. 5
Ezekiel 34:4, p. 15
Ezekiel 36:26, p. 133
Ezekiel 44:21, p. 56

Genesis 1:28, p. 111
Genesis 2:18, p. 111
Genesis 3:12–13, p. 85
Genesis 18:20–21, p. 154
Genesis 32:26, p. 115

Hosea 4:6, p. 29

Isaiah 1:3, p. 148
Isaiah 1:11–12, 17, p. 16
Isaiah 1:13, p. 150
Isaiah 1:15, p. 150
Isaiah 1:16, p. 150
Isaiah 1:18, p. 150
Isaiah 3:1–3, p. 136
Isaiah 30:8, p. 13
Isaiah 41:26, p. 13
Isaiah 45:11, p. 88
Isaiah 56:10, p. 6
Isaiah 58: 1, p. 21
Isaiah 58:4–9, p. 144
Isaiah 65:12, p. 149

Jeremiah 2:8 (NKJV), p. 6
Jeremiah 3:15, p. 4
Jeremiah 4:17–18, p. 154
Jeremiah 6:9, p. 141
Jeremiah 7:13, p. 149
Jeremiah 10:17 LXX, p. 157
Jeremiah 11:7–8, p. 149
Jeremiah 14:7, p. 156
Jeremiah 23:1, p. 7
Jeremiah 30:2, p. 13
Jeremiah 48:10 (NKJV), p. 74
Joel 2:12–13, p. 156
Joel 2:15–16 (NKJV), p. 142
Joel 2:17, p. xvii, 156
Joel 2:18–20, p. 142
Joshua 1:8, p. 29

1 Kings 1:13,15 LXX, p. 124
1 Kings 3:11–14 LXX, p. 60
1 Kings 6 LXX, p. 156
1 Kings 7:6 LXX, p. 141
1 Kings 12:23, p. 160
1 Kings 15:22 LXX, p. 166
1 Kings 15:23 LXX, p. 166

Lamentations 3:37 LXX, p. 126
Leviticus 8, p. 29
Leviticus 10, p. 160
Leviticus 10:9, p. 56
Leviticus 16:29–31, p. 141
Leviticus 16:34, p. xvii, 151
Leviticus 19:30, p. x
Leviticus 22:2, p. x

Malachi 2:7, p. xiv

2 Maccabees 12:41–46, p. 159

Nehemiah 2:4, p. 124
Nehemiah 9:1, 3, p. 141
Nehemiah 9:2, p. 86
Numbers 5:7, p. 86

Numbers 11:2, p. 156
Numbers 15:25, p. 151
Numbers 15:27–30, p. 20
Numbers 15:30, p. 91
Numbers 17:13 LXX, p. 156

Proverbs 1:25–30 LXX, p. 149
Proverbs 8:14, p. 136
Proverbs 27:25 LXX, p. 60
Proverbs 28:13, p. 86
Proverbs 30:5, p. 4
Psalm 5:2, p. 125
Psalm 5:5, p. 129
Psalm 6:1–4, p. 133
Psalm 18:2–3 LXX, p. 123
Psalm 28 LXX, p. 164
Psalm 28:1 LXX, p. 130
Psalm 28:9 LXX, p. 165
Psalm 36:3–4, p. 85
Psalm 41:2–5 LXX, p. 165
Psalm 49:16, p. 38
Psalm 45:1 LXX, p. 155
Psalm 46:7–8 LXX, p. 165
Psalm 49:15 LXX, p. 155
Psalm 49:16, p. 33, 37
Psalm 50:17 LXX, p. 148
Psalm 72:25–26 LXX, p. 131
Psalm 76:7, p. 124
Psalm 77:11 LXX, p. 157
Psalm 83:2–3 LXX, p. 165
Psalm 85:5 LXX, p. 146
Psalm 91:16 LXX, p. 147
Psalm 98:3, p. 129
Psalm 98:6–7, p. 156
Psalm 99:3 LXX, p. 150
Psalm 99:4 LXX, p. 164
Psalm 99:5 LXX, p. 97
Psalm 100:5,10 LXX, p. 85
Psalm 102:1–2 LXX, p. 130
Psalm 103:28 LXX, p. 157
Psalm 105:23 LXX, p. 156
Psalm 110:8, p. 123

Psalm 118:18 LXX, p. 28
Psalm 118:25,28,29 LXX, p. 132
Psalm 118:34 LXX, p. 28
Psalm 118:35, p. 5
Psalm 138:2–3 LXX, p. 139
Psalm 144: 9 LXX, p. 157
Psalm 144:13 LXX, p. 134
Psalm 144:15 LXX, p. 136
Psalm 144:18 LXX, p. 146
Psalm 144:19 LXX, p. 148

2 Samuel 12:11–13, p. 117

Sirach 1:23, p. 90
Sirach 2:11, p. 90
Sirach 5:7, p. 84

Tobit 8:7, p. 112

Zechariah 7, p. 144
Zechariah 8, p. 144
Zechariah 10:1, p. 155

The New Testament

Acts 1:24, p. 125
Acts 2:21, p. 147
Acts 3:1, p. 165
Acts 4:12, p. 25
Acts 4:24, p. 125
Acts 4:29, p. 152
Acts 5:41, p. 158
Acts 6:4, p. xvii, 151
Acts 10–11, p. 58
Acts 10:43, p. 25
Acts 13:2, p. 142
Acts 14:22–24, p. 152
Acts 16:14, p. 17
Acts 16:25, p. 158
Acts 17:28, p. 157
Acts 19:18, p. 86
Acts 20:18, p. 31

Acts 20:19, p. 97
Acts 20:19, 31, p. 22, 31
Acts 20:20, p. 26, 30, 31
Acts 20:21, p. 9, 30
Acts 20:24, p. 31
Acts 20:26, p. 31
Acts 20:27, p. 30
Acts 20:28, p. 5
Acts 20:31, p. 22, 26, 31
Acts 20:33, p. 31, 59
Acts 20:34, p. 31
Acts 20:35, p. 53
Acts 20:36, p. 153
Acts 24:10–21, p. 58
Acts 25:8, p. 58
Acts 26:2–30, p. 58

Colossians 1:13, p. 135
Colossians 1:14, p. 90
Colossians 1:28, p. 26
Colossians 3:5, p. 25, 59, 139
Colossians 3:16, p. 29, 124
Colossians 4:2, p. 139
Colossians 4:3, p. 152

1 Corinthians 1:23–24, p. 26
1 Corinthians 1:30, p. 25
1 Corinthians 2:3, p. xi
1 Corinthians 3:9, p. xiv
1 Corinthians 3:10, p. xiv
1 Corinthians 4:1, p. xvii
1 Corinthians 4:2, p. 68
1 Corinthians 4:12, p. 64
1 Corinthians 4:12–13, p. 58
1 Corinthians 4:15, p. 5
1 Corinthians 6:10, p. 56
1 Corinthians 6: 20, p. 125
1 Corinthians 7:5, p. 141
1 Corinthians 7:5, 29, p. 111
1 Corinthians 8: 12, p. 57
1 Corinthians 9:7, p. 74
1 Corinthians 9:14, p. 74

1 Corinthians 9:16–17, p. 3
1 Corinthians 9:20, p. 66
1 Corinthians 9:22, p. 66
1 Corinthians 9:26–27,
    p. 35, 66
1 Corinthians 10:6, p. 90
1 Corinthians 11:1, p. 35
1 Corinthians 11:24, p. 161
1 Corinthians 11:24–26, p. 99
1 Corinthians 11:27, p. 162
1 Corinthians 11:28, p. 100
1 Corinthians 11:29, p. 162
1 Corinthians 14:15, p. 124
1 Corinthians 16:1, p. 53

2 Corinthians 1:20, p. 130
2 Corinthians 1:4–5, p. 24
2 Corinthians 2:4, p. 22
2 Corinthians 2:7–8, p. 24
2 Corinthians 3:6, p. 160
2 Corinthians 3:8–9, p. x
2 Corinthians 3:16, p. 135
2 Corinthians 4: 5, p. 97
2 Corinthians 5:18, p. x
2 Corinthians 6:14–15, p. 100
2 Corinthians 7:1, p. 73, 130
2 Corinthians 8:19, p. 53
2 Corinthians 10:4, p. 4
2 Corinthians 11:2, p. 5
2 Corinthians 11:29, p. 22
2 Corinthians 12:21, p. 22
2 Corinthians 13:10, p. 97
2 Corinthians 15:18–19, p. xiv

Ephesians 1:7, p. 90
Ephesians 1:16–17, p. 17, 153
Ephesians 2:18, p. 146
Ephesians 2:8–9, p. 116
Ephesians 2:8–10, p. 17
Ephesians 3:14, p. 130
Ephesians 3:16, p. 130
Ephesians 3:17, p. 97, 157

Ephesians 3:19, p. 130, 157
Ephesians 4:1, p. 9
Ephesians 4:8–11, p. xiii
Ephesians 4:12–13, p. xiv
Ephesians 4:30, p. 133
Ephesians 4:32, p. 136
Ephesians 5:1, p. 136
Ephesians 5:17, p. 4
Ephesians 5:20, p. 158
Ephesians 5:22–33, p. 111
Ephesians 5:32, p. 112
Ephesians 6:18, p. 125, 140

Galatians 1:11–12, p. 12
Galatians 2:10, p. 53
Galatians 3:13, p. 85
Galatians 4:17, p. 19
Galatians 4:19, p. 5, 22, 91
Galatians 5:21, p. 56
Galatians 5:22, p. 135
Galatians 6:1–2, p. 22

Hebrews 1:1, p. 12
Hebrews 2:2, p. x
Hebrews 4:12, p. 4
Hebrews 4:14, p. 152
Hebrews 5:2–4, p. 151
Hebrews 6:4, p. 91
Hebrews 6:4, p. 20
Hebrews 10:14, p. 95
Hebrews 10:22, p. 172
Hebrews 10:23, p. 146
Hebrews 10:26, p. 20
Hebrews 10:26,29, p. 91
Hebrews 11:2, p. 131
Hebrews 11:6, p. 73
Hebrews 12: 29, p. 129
Hebrews 12:2, p. 25
Hebrews 12:22–24, p. 163
Hebrews 12:28, p. 41
Hebrews 12:28–29, p. xi
Hebrews 13:4, p. 112

James 1:6–7, p. 149
James 1:13–14, p. 25
James 1:15, p. 25
James 1:17, p. 121
James 1:21, p. 145
James 1:25, p. 84
James 2:10, p. 23
James 2:20, p. 23
James 3:2, p. 154
James 4:1, p. 144
James 4:3, p. 149
James 5:14, p. xvii, 152
James 5:14–15, p. 115, 140
James 5:15, p. 155
James 5:16, p. 140
John 1:1, p. 146
John 1:29, p. 26
John 1:9, p. 86
John 3: 16, p. 116
John 3:16, p. 90, 130
John 3:27, p. 121
John 3:29, p. 5
John 4:23, p. 122, 126
John 4:23–24, p. 124
John 4:24, p. 16, 41, 127
John 5: 24, p. 117
John 5:35, p. 35
John 6:29, p. 135
John 6:40, p. 117
John 6:51, p. 160
John 6:54, p. 99
John 6:56, p. 162
John 6:58, p. 162
John 8:46, p. 33
John 9:31, p. 129
John 10, p. 30
John 10:4, p. 35
John 10:10, p. xvi
John 10:15, p. 26
John 10:28–29, p. 137
John 12:48, p. 17
John 12:6, p. 59

John 13:2,27, p. 59
John 14:6, p. 26
John 14:13–14, p. 7
John 15:4, p. 66
John 15:7, p. 7, 172
John 15:15, p. xiv
John 15:16, p. 66
John 15:22, p. 17
John 16:13, p. x
John 16:23, p. 148, 151
John 16:24, p. 121, 151
John 17: 11, p. 152
John 17: 15, p. 152
John 17: 17, p. 152
John 17: 19, p. 152
John 17: 20, p. 152
John 17: 8, p. 152
John 17:3, p. 26
John 18:36, p. 97
John 21:15, p. xvi

1 John 1:7, p. 90, 116
1 John 2: 2, p. 90, 115
1 John 2:15, p. 24
1 John 4:1, p. 12
1 John 5:14, p. 148
1 John 5:16, p. 20, 91, 154

Jude 1: 12, p. 28

Luke 2:37, p. 142, 165
Luke 4:23, p. 33
Luke 5:16, p. 124
Luke 5:33–35, p. 142
Luke 5:5, p. 23
Luke 6:12, p. 124
Luke 7:38, p. 117
Luke 9:54, p. 19
Luke 10:34, p. 22
Luke 11:1, p. 164
Luke 11:2, p. 125
Luke 11:2–4, p. 134

Luke 11:13, p. 7, 147
Luke 12:37, p. 139
Luke 12:42, p. 68
Luke 13:7, p. 89
Luke 13:24, p. 131
Luke 14, p. 86
Luke 15:4, p. 27
Luke 15:7, p. 140
Luke 15:10, p. 140
Luke 15:11, p. 117
Luke 15:21, p. 138
Luke 17:13, p. 138
Luke 17:18, p. 157
Luke 18:9, p. 117
Luke 18:11, p. 86, 149
Luke 18:13, p. 130, 138
Luke 19:13, p. 66
Luke 21:19, p. 66
Luke 21:34, p. 140, 145
Luke 21: 34,36, p. 40
Luke 22:14, p. 160
Luke 22:19, p. 99
Luke 22:32, p. 153
Luke 22:46, p. 151
Luke 22:61, p. 117
Luke 23:42, p. 117, 138
Luke 24:45, p. 17
Luke 24:47, p. 25

Mark 1:15, p. 9
Mark 2:7, p. 97
Mark 7:23, p. 25
Mark 10:38, p. 129
Mark 11:14, p. 89
Mark 11:25, p. 148
Mark 12:30, p. 130
Mark 13:33, p. 144
Mark 13:37, p. 144
Mark 16:15–16, p. 3
Mark 21, p. 89
Matthew 3:6, p. 86
Matthew 3:10, p. 89

Matthew 4:10, p. 150
Matthew 5:4, p. 24
Matthew 5:13, p. xiv
Matthew 5:14, p. xiv
Matthew 5:16, p. xiv, xvi, 34
Matthew 5:19, p. 34
Matthew 5:23–24, p. 87
Matthew 5:44, p. 140
Matthew 6:5, p. 149
Matthew 6:6, p. 124
Matthew 6:9, p. 121
Matthew 6:14–15, p. 136
Matthew 6:15, p. 149
Matthew 6:16–18, p. 142
Matthew 7:5, p. 33
Matthew 7:6, p. 73
Matthew 7:7, p. 121
Matthew 7:13–14, p. 23
Matthew 8:8, p. 138
Matthew 8:9, p. 130
Matthew 9:13, p. 90, 116
Matthew 9:14–15, p. 142
Matthew 9:16, p. 22
Matthew 9:38, p. 152
Matthew 10:8, p. 59, 74
Matthew 10:10, p. 74
Matthew 10:16, p. 66
Matthew 12: 31–32, p. 91
Matthew 12:44–45, p. 144
Matthew 13:22, p. 17
Matthew 14:23, p. 124
Matthew 15:16, p. 21
Matthew 15:19–20, p. 40
Matthew 15:8, p. 126
Matthew 18:15–16, p. 20
Matthew 18:19–20, p. 164
Matthew 18:35, p. 87
Matthew 20:1, 6, p. 23
Matthew 20:25–27, p. 97
Matthew 21: 22, p. 148
Matthew 21:13, p. 165
Matthew 22:3, p. 5

Matthew 22:37, p. 122
Matthew 24:4, p. 144
Matthew 24:42, p. 144
Matthew 24:48–51, p. xv
Matthew 24:49, p. 57
Matthew 24:50–51, p. 4, 68
Matthew 24:51, p. x
Matthew 25, p. 90
Matthew 25:10–13, p. 145
Matthew 25:25, p. 6
Matthew 25:30, p. xv
Matthew 26:26, p. 160
Matthew 26:39–42, p. 125
Matthew 28:19, p. 3
Matthew 28:19–20, p. xiii

1 Peter 1:6–7, p. 24
1 Peter 1:13, p. 145
1 Peter 1:16, p. 130
1 Peter 2:11, p. 24, 25
1 Peter 2:14, p. 153
1 Peter 2:19–20, p. 25
1 Peter 2:23, p. 58
1 Peter 3:14, p. 24
1 Peter 3:21, p. 77
1 Peter 3:5–7, p. 111
1 Peter 4:17–18, p. 89
1 Peter 4:7, p. 140
1 Peter 5:2–3, p. xiv, 35
1 Peter 5:8, p. 40, 144
1 Peter 5:8–9, p. 24
1 Peter 2:1, p. 145
1 Peter 4:16, p. 25

2 Peter 1:11, p. 135
2 Peter 1:20–21, p. 12
2 Peter 2:4–6, p. 90
2 Peter 2:17, p. 6
2 Peter 2:22, p. 86
Philippians 2:21, p. 6, 68
Philippians 3:13–14, p. 67
Philippians 3:17, p. 35, 36, 67

Philippians 3:18, p. 22
Philippians 3:20–21, p. 117

Revelation 2:1, p. xiv
Revelation 2:8, p. xiv
Revelation 2:12, p. xiv
Revelation 2:18, p. xiv
Revelation 3:1, p. xiv
Revelation 3:7, p. xiv
Revelation 3:14, p. xiv
Romans 1:9–10, p. 153
Romans 1:16, p. 4
Romans 2:21–24, p. 37
Romans 2:4–5, p. 88
Romans 2:6, p. 26
Romans 2:6–7, p. 139
Romans 3:20, p. 84
Romans 3:24–25, p. 116
Romans 4:20–21, p. 131
Romans 4:25, p. 115
Romans 5:1, p. 86
Romans 6:6, p. 154
Romans 6:12, p. 91
Romans 6:12–14, p. 154
Romans 6:14, p. 135
Romans 6:16, p. 87, 91
Romans 6:19, p. 154
Romans 7:7, p. 84
Romans 7:14–15, p. 139
Romans 7:24, p. 25
Romans 8:1, p. 86
Romans 8:2, p. 139
Romans 8:23, p. 124
Romans 8:26, p. 133, 146
Romans 8:32, p. 157
Romans 8:34, p. 146
Romans 8:35, p. 125, 130
Romans 8:38–39, p. 131
Romans 10:2, p. 19
Romans 10:14, p. 3, 71
Romans 10:17, p. 71
Romans 12:1, p. 16, 122

Romans 12:1–2, p. 146
Romans 13:1, p. 136
Romans 13:3–4, p. 153
Romans 14:17, p. 100
Romans 14:23, p. 73
Romans 15:13, p. 100
Romans 15:4, p. 15

1 Thessalonians 2:11, p. 22
1 Thessalonians 3:1–3, p. 140
1 Thessalonians 4:3–7, p. 111
1 Thessalonians 4:4–7, p. 144
1 Thessalonians 5:6, p. 144
1 Thessalonians 5:17, p. 139
1 Thessalonians 5:18, p. 157
1 Thessalonians 5:21–22, p. 12
2 Thessalonians, p. 160
2 Thessalonians 1:8, p. 26
2 Thessalonians 3:15, p. 19
1 Timothy 1:19–20, p. 23
1 Timothy 2:1, p. 157
1 Timothy 2:1–2, p. xvii, 152
1 Timothy 2:2–3, p. 153
1 Timothy 2:4, p. 135
1 Timothy 2:5–6, p. 146
1 Timothy 2:8, p. 148
1 Timothy 3, p. xvi
1 Timothy 3:4, p. 60
1 Timothy 3:5, p. 60
1 Timothy 3:8, p. 65
1 Timothy 3:11, p. 60
1 Timothy 3:14–15, p. 67
1 Timothy 4:6, p. 4, 28
1 Timothy 4:7, p. 16
1 Timothy 4:8, p. 138
1 Timothy 4:12, p. 35
1 Timothy 4:13, 15, p. 29
1 Timothy 5:20, p. 20
1 Timothy 5:21, p. xci

1 Timothy 6:4–5, p. 57
1 Timothy 6:11–12, p. 59
1 Timothy 6:17, p. 130
1 Timothy 14; 6:6:2, p. 4
2 Timothy 1:13, p. 6
2 Timothy 2:2, p. 4, 30
2 Timothy 2:14, p. 57
2 Timothy 2:15, p. 68
2 Timothy 2:21, p. 97
2 Timothy 2:24, p. 3
2 Timothy 2:24–25, p. 18, 97
2 Timothy 2:24–25; 2, p. 19
2 Timothy 2:25, p. 22
2 Timothy 24:3, p. 4
2 Timothy 3:15, p. 5
2 Timothy 3:15–17, p. 7
2 Timothy 3:16–17, p. 15
2 Timothy 4:1, p. xvi
2 Timothy 4:1–2, p. 3
2 Timothy 4:2, p. ix, 26
2 Timothy 4:5, p. 4
2 Timothy 4:8, p. 139
2 Timothy 14–15, p. 4

Titus 1, p. xvi
Titus 1:6, p. 60
Titus 1:7, p. 64
Titus 1:7–9. ix
Titus 1:8, p. 39
Titus 1:9, p. 55
Titus 15; 3:8, p. 4
Titus 1:13, p. 19
Titus 2:1, p. 4
Titus 2:12, p. 67
Titus 2:12–13, p. 9
Titus 2:7–8, p. 35
Titus 3:10, p. 19
Titus 7, p. 4